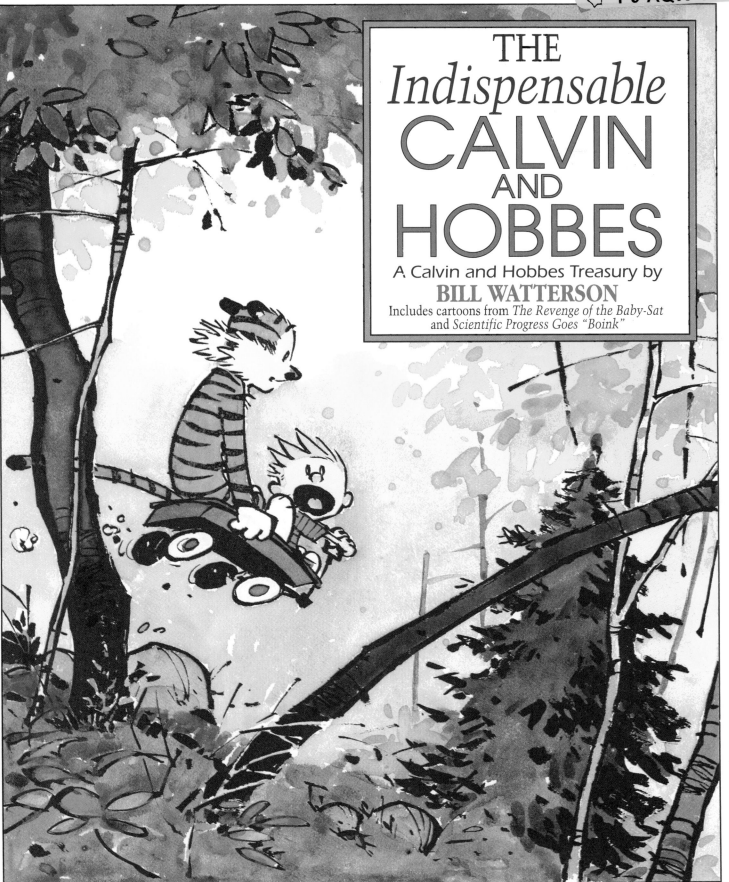

THE
Indispensable
CALVIN
AND
HOBBES

A Calvin and Hobbes Treasury by
BILL WATTERSON
Includes cartoons from *The Revenge of the Baby-Sat*
and *Scientific Progress Goes "Boink"*

Andrews McMeel
Publishing, LLC

Kansas City • Sydney • London

Andrews McMeel Publishing, LLC
an Andrews McMeel Universal company
1130 Walnut Street, Kansas City, Missouri 64106

www.andrewsmcmeel.com

ISBN: 978-1-4494-3707-7

Library of Congress Control Number: 92-72247 (paperback)
92-72248 (hardback)

15 16 17 18 19 SDB 10 9 8 7 6 5 4 3

I made a big decision a little while ago.
I don't remember what it was, which prob'ly goes to show
That many times a simple choice can prove to be essential
Even though it often might appear inconsequential.

I must have been distracted when I left my home because
Left or right I'm sure I went. (I wonder which it was!)
Anyway, I never veered: I walked in that direction
Utterly absorbed, it seems, in quiet introspection.

For no reason I can think of, I've wandered far astray.
And that is how I got to where I find myself today.

Explorers are we, intrepid and bold,
Out in the wild, amongst wonders untold.
Equipped with our wits, a map, and a snack,
We're searching for fun and we're on the right track!

My mother has eyes on the back of her head!
I don't quite believe it, but that's what she said.
She explained that she'd been so uniquely endowed
To catch me when I did Things Not Allowed.
I think she must also have eyes on her rear.
I've noticed her hindsight is unusually clear.

At night my mind does not much care
If what it thinks is here or there.
It tells me stories it invents
And makes up things that don't make sense.
I don't know why it does this stuff.
The real world seems quite weird enough.

What if my bones were in a museum,
Where aliens paid good money to see 'em?
And suppose that they'd put me together all wrong,
Sticking bones on to bones where they didn't belong!

Imagine phalanges, pelvis, and spine
Welded to mandibles that once had been mine!
With each misassemblage, the error compounded,
The aliens would draw back in terror, astounded!

Their textbooks would show me in grim illustration,
The most hideous thing ever seen in creation!
The museum would commission a model in plaster
Of ME, to be called, "Evolution's Disaster"!

And paleontologists there would debate
Dozens of theories to help postulate
How man survived for those thousands of years
With teeth-covered arms growing out of his ears!

Oh, I hope that I'm never in such manner displayed,
No matter HOW much to see me the aliens paid.

I did not want to go with them.
Alas, I had no choice.
This was made quite clear to me
In threat'ning tones of voice.

I protested mightily
And scrambled 'cross the floor.
But though I grabbed the furniture,
They dragged me out the door.

In the car, I screamed and moaned.
I cried my red eyes dry.
The window down, I yelled for help
To people we passed by.

Mom and Dad can make the rules
And certain things forbid,
But I can make them wish that they
Had never had a kid.

Now I'm in bed,
The sheets pulled to my head.
My tiger is here making Zs.
He's furry and hot.
He takes up a lot
Of the bed and he's hogging the breeze.

WHO MADE THIS MESS OUT HERE?!

IT WASN'T *ME*, MOM! IT WAS...UH.. IT WAS...

IT WAS A HORRIBLE LITTLE VENUSIAN WHO MATERIALIZED IN THE KITCHEN! HE TOOK OUT SOME DIABOLICAL HIGH-FREQUENCY DEVICE, POINTED IT AT VARIOUS OBJECTS, AND...

MOTHERS ARE THE NECESSITY OF INVENTION.

I'M HO-OME!

KAP-OW!

WHAT DID YOU DO, STEP ON A LAND MINE?

WHEN'S DAD EVER GOING TO BUILD THAT TIGER PIT I KEEP ASKING HIM ABOUT?

CALVIN, WHERE ARE YOU? GET OUT HERE!

COME ON, CALVIN, I'M GETTING TIRED OF THIS!

I *MEAN* IT, CALVIN! COME OUT AND TAKE YOUR BATH! *NOW!*

SOONER OR LATER SHE'S GOING TO HAVE TO QUESTION WHETHER THIS IS REALLY WORTH THE TROUBLE.

CALVIN AND HOBBES
by WATTERSON

IF *I* WAS IN CHARGE, WE'D NEVER SEE GRASS BETWEEN OCTOBER AND MAY.

ON "THREE," READY? ONE... TWO... THREE!

SNOW!

I SAID SNOW! C'MON! SNOW!

SNOW!

OK THEN, *DON'T* SNOW! SEE WHAT *I* CARE! I *LIKE* THIS WEATHER! LET'S HAVE IT FOREVER!

PLEEAASE SNOW! PLEASE?? JUST A FOOT! OK, EIGHT INCHES! THAT'S ALL! C'MON! SIX INCHES, EVEN! HOW ABOUT JUST SIX??

I'M *WAAIIITING...*

RRRRGGGHHH

DO YOU WANT ME TO BECOME AN ATHEIST?

SPIFF'S SPACECRAFT IS IMMOBILIZED! THE NAVIGA-TRON HAS SHORTED OUT!

A ZILLION MILES FROM ANY PLANET, OUR HERO MUST CLIMB OUT AND FIX IT HIMSELF IN ZERO GRAVITY!

UPSIDE DOWN, SPIFF CLINGS TIGHTLY TO HIS SPACE SHIP! ONE SLIP WILL SEND HIM HURLING INTO THE HORRORS OF THE INFINITE BEYOND!

GO...TO...SCHOOL!

NO!

I DON'T UNDERSTAND HOW SANTA RUNS HIS OPERATION. HOW CAN HE AFFORD TO GIVE TOYS AWAY?

HOW DOES HE PAY FOR THE RAW MATERIALS HE USES TO MAKE THE TOYS? HOW DOES HE PAY HIS ELVES?

THERE'S NO INCOME TO COVER HIS COSTS. HOW DOES HE DO IT?

DEFICIT SPENDING, I GUESS.

SURE, BUT SOONER OR LATER IT'S GOING TO CATCH UP TO HIM, AND THEN WHERE WILL I BE?!

DEAR SANTA, Hi, it's ME, CALViN. THiS YEAR I'VE BEEN

EXTRA GOOD, SO... PBTBT!!

MMF MMF EEP!

PERHAPS YOU NEED A DRINK OF WATER.

I THINK I DO.

14

I'm gonna pound you in gym class, shrimp.

GET YOUR KICKS **NOW**, YOU GLANDULAR FREAK, BECAUSE ONCE YOU GROW UP YOU CAN'T GO BEATING PEOPLE UP FOR NO REASON!

Yeah, I guess you're right.

THAT REALLY WASN'T WHAT I MEANT AT ALL.

WHAT GRADE DID YOU GET?

I GOT AN "A."

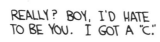
REALLY? BOY, I'D HATE TO BE YOU. I GOT A "C."

WHY ON EARTH WOULD YOU RATHER GET A "C" THAN AN "A"?!

I FIND MY LIFE IS A LOT EASIER THE LOWER I KEEP EVERYONE'S EXPECTATIONS.

WHY DO I HAVE TO WEAR THESE DORKY CLOTHES AND GET MY HAIR COMBED?!

YOUR DAD'S GOING TO TAKE YOUR PICTURE. HOLD STILL.

I DON'T **WANT** TO GET MY PICTURE TAKEN!

IT WILL JUST TAKE A FEW MINUTES. WE'RE GOING TO PUT THE PICTURE OF YOU IN OUR CHRISTMAS CARDS SO EVERYONE CAN SEE WHAT YOU LOOK LIKE NOW.

WHAT A DUMB IDEA. WHY ARE WE DOING *THAT*?

SO WE WON'T HAVE RELATIVES DROPPING BY TO VISIT.

DEAR...

CALVIN and HOBBES

by WATTERSON

AHH... THE PERFECT SLUSHBALL!

HARD ENOUGH TO STING, YET SLOPPY ENOUGH TO DRIBBLE DOWN THE COLLAR AND SOAK THE UNDERGARMENTS.

HERE COMES SUSIE! NOW'S MY CHANCE TO HIT HER WITH A SLUSHBALL!

I SEE YOU! YOU'D BETTER NOT THROW THAT! SANTA CLAUS IS WATCHING YOU RIGHT NOW!

FWISSHHH!

ZINGG

WHAP!

OH YES! YES! IT WAS WORTH IT! WHAT A SHOT! I'M NOT SORRY! OH, IT WAS BEAUTIFUL! I'D DO IT AGAIN IN A MINUTE! HA HA!

SANTA'S GONNA SKIP THIS BLOCK FOR YEARS.

DO YOU THINK MONSTERS ARE UNDER THE BED TONIGHT?

I DON'T KNOW. HOW CAN YOU TELL WITHOUT LOOKING?

ONE WAY IS TO TELL A STORY ABOUT A LITTLE KID GETTING MAULED AND EATEN ALIVE.

HOW DOES *THAT* TELL YOU IF YOU HAVE MONSTERS?

SOMETIMES THEY LAUGH.

I'M FREEZING! WHY DO WE KEEP THIS HOUSE SO DARN COLD?!

CRANK UP THE THERMOSTAT AND BUILD A FIRE, WILL YA?

I HAVE A BETTER IDEA. C'MERE.

OK, STEP OUTSIDE.

WHY? WHAT'S OUTSIDE?

IN A FEW MINUTES YOU CAN COME IN, AND THEN THE HOUSE WILL SEEM NICE AND WARM.

I'M TELLING THE NEWSPAPERS ABOUT YOU, DAD!

READ ME "HAMSTER HUEY AND THE GOOEY KABLOOIE."

OH, I DON'T WANT TO READ THAT AGAIN. LET'S READ SOMETHING DIFFERENT TONIGHT.

NO, I WANT TO HEAR "HAMSTER HUEY AND THE GOOEY KABLOOIE."

C'MON, CALVIN, I'VE READ THIS A THOUSAND TIMES.

READ IT AGAIN. PLEASE? *PLEASE*?

ALL RIGHT, ALL RIGHT.

YOU'LL DO THE SQUEAKY VOICES, THE GOOSHY SOUND EFFECTS, AND THE HAPPY HAMSTER HOP, WON'T YOU?

LOOK, CAN'T WE READ SOMETHING ELSE?

MOMM! MOM!

WHAT IS IT? WHAT'S THE MATTER?

DO PEOPLE GROW FROM SPORES?

SPORES?!? YOU WAKE ME UP AT 2 AM. TO ASK IF PEOPLE GROW FROM *SPORES*? ARE YOU OUT OF YOUR MIND?? WHY ARE YOU EVEN AWAKE?! GO TO SLEEP!!

SHE DIDN'T ANSWER. SHE MUST NOT KNOW.

I'M TELLING YOU, IT'S TRUE.

I SAY IT'S A FALLACY THAT KIDS NEED 12 YEARS OF SCHOOL! THREE MONTHS IS PLENTY!

LOOK AT ME. I'M SMART! I DON'T NEED 11½ MORE YEARS OF SCHOOL! IT'S A COMPLETE WASTE OF MY TIME!

HOW ON EARTH DID YOU GET ALL THE WAY TO THE BUS STOP WITH BOTH FEET THROUGH ONE PANT LEG?

I FELL DOWN A LOT.

... WHY? WHAT'S YOUR POINT?

NOTHING. I WAS JUST CURIOUS.

HOW'S MY PEANUT BUTTER SANDWICH COMING? YOU'RE USING CHUNKY PEANUT BUTTER, RIGHT? I WON'T EAT SMOOTH!

MAKE IT AN OPEN FACE SAND-WICH, TOO! DON'T PUT ANY JELLY ON IT OR ANYTHING! AND USE SOME NORMAL BREAD! I DON'T LIKE THOSE WEIRD GRAIN BREADS!

DID YOU CUT IT DIAGONALLY? I LIKE TRIANGLES BETTER THAN RECTANGLES, SO BE SURE TO CUT IT RIGHT!

YOUR MAJESTY'S SANDWICH.

HEY, THIS IS A CLOSED-FACE, HORIZONTALLY CUT, SMOOTH PEANUT BUTTER SANDWICH ON WEIRD BREAD WITH JELLY! WEREN'T YOU *LISTENING*?!

THERE'S NOTHING PRETTIER THAN NEW FALLEN SNOW ON A CLEAR, FREEZING MOONLIT NIGHT.

... THROUGH A WINDOW, THAT IS.

I CAN'T TAKE A BATH IN THIS! THE WATER'S *BOILING*! I'LL SCALD MYSELF!

WHAT ARE YOU TRYING TO DO, COOK ME ALIVE?? WELL, FORGET IT! I'M NOT GETTING IN!

BY THE TIME YOU QUIT FUSSING, COMPLAINING, YELLING AND SCREAMING, AND ACTUALLY TAKE OFF YOUR CLOTHES AND GET IN, THE WATER WILL BE PERFECT!

BOY, DOES SHE KNOW ME.

EVERY DAY I HAVE TO GET UP AND GO TO SCHOOL.

NOTHING EVER CHANGES. IT'S JUST SCHOOL, SCHOOL, SCHOOL.

BUT NOT TODAY.

TODAY, I GO FOR THE GUSTO.

I THINK YOU SHOULD ASK YOUR MOM IF IT'S OK.

BOY, DID I GET IN TROUBLE AT SCHOOL TODAY. WOW.

WHAT HAPPENED?

I DON'T EVEN WANT TO TALK ABOUT IT.

DID IT HAVE ANYTHING TO DO WITH ALL THOSE SIRENS ABOUT NOON?

I *SAID* I DON'T WANT TO TALK ABOUT IT.

DID YOU BRING SOMETHING FOR SHOW AND TELL?

YOU BET!

I BROUGHT THESE CHARRED ROCKS AND ASHES FROM MY BACK YARD.

SEE? DRAMATIC PROOF THAT UFOs LANDED NOT A HUNDRED FEET FROM MY HOUSE! THEIR RETRO ROCKETS BURNED SOLID ROCK INTO THIS FRAGILE GRAY DUST CUBE!

THIS IS AN OLD CHARCOAL BRIQUETTE.

EVEN AS WE SPEAK, ALIENS ARE UNDOUBTEDLY INFILTRATING THE HIGHEST LEVELS OF OUR GOVERNMENT.

DISGUSTING DENIZEN OF THE DEEP, THE GIANT OCTOPUS GLIDES ACROSS THE OCEAN FLOOR.

AT THE SIGHT OF AN ENEMY, HE RELEASES A CLOUD OF INK AND MAKES HIS GETAWAY!

MISS WORMWOOD!

SHOVEL, SHOVEL, SHOVEL!

WHY CAN'T WE GET A SNOW BLOWER?? WE MUST BE THE ONLY FAMILY IN THE WORLD THAT STILL SHOVELS THE DRIVEWAY BY HAND! I'M FREEZING!

IT BUILDS CHARACTER. KEEP AT IT.

PRETTY CONVENIENT HOW EVERY TIME *I* BUILD CHARACTER, *HE* SAVES A COUPLE HUNDRED DOLLARS.

NEXT TIME WE GO DOWN, *I* GET TO STEER THE SLED.

YOU?! YOU STEER LIKE AN OLD LADY!

YEAH, WELL, I'M SICK OF GOING OVER AND THROUGH EVERY OBSTACLE ON THE HILL.

"EVERY OBSTACLE"?!? WE MISSED THE BRIAR PATCH, DIDN'T WE?!

BY GOING DOWN THE GULLY AND INTO THE STREAM, YES.

OH, YOU MAKE EVERYTHING SOUND SO TERRIBLE. YOU SHOULD BE GLAD WE'RE ALIVE.

THIS IS THE FINEST SNOWBALL EVER MADE!

PAINSTAKINGLY HAND-CRAFTED INTO A PERFECT SPHERE FROM A SECRET MIXTURE OF SLUSH, ICE, DIRT, DEBRIS AND FINE POWDER SNOW, THIS *IS* THE ULTIMATE WINTER WEAPON!

YES, THIS MARVEL OF CRYSTALLINE ENGINEERING WI..

WHAP!!

ANOTHER CASUALTY OF THE SEDUCTION OF ART.

WHAT DO YOU THINK IS THE BEST WAY TO GET WHAT YOU WANT? IS IT BETTER TO HOLD FAST AND NEVER BACK DOWN, OR TO COMPROMISE?

I SUPPOSE IT'S BEST TO HOLD FAST WHEN YOU CAN, AND COMPROMISE WHEN YOU NEED TO.

THAT'S A LOT MORE MATURE THAN I THINK I CARE TO BE.

I THINK THE SHORT ATTENTION SPAN OF TELEVISION IS GREAT.

AS FAR AS *I'M* CONCERNED, IF SOMETHING IS SO COMPLICATED THAT YOU CAN'T EXPLAIN IT IN 10 SECONDS, THEN IT'S PROBABLY NOT WORTH KNOWING ANYWAY.

MY TIME IS VALUABLE. I CAN'T GO THINKING ABOUT ONE SUBJECT FOR MINUTES ON END. I'M A BUSY MAN.

...WHO'S BEEN SITTING HERE FOR THREE HOURS.

... AT SIX THOUGHTS A MINUTE.

THERE'S SOMETHING MAGICAL ABOUT HAVING A FIRE.

THE CRACKLES AND SNAPS, THE WARM, FLICKERING LIGHT... EVERYTHING ALWAYS SEEMS SAFE AND COZY IF YOU'RE SITTING IN FRONT OF A FIRE.

AND IF YOU'VE GOT A HOT TIGER TUMMY TO LIE AGAINST.... *WELL!*

CALVIN and HOBBES
by WATTERSON

HOW COME?

C'MON, WE'D BETTER GO OUTSIDE FOR A WHILE.

MOM'S GETTING THAT LOOK.

THIS WILL BE THE BEST SNOW FORT EVER BUILT!

OK, THE MAIN FORTRESS WILL BE A WALL FIVE FEET HIGH, AND GO FROM HERE DOWN OVER THAT HILL, WITH TURRETS EVERY 50 FEET.

OVER HERE WE'LL BUILD AN INNER WALL, IN CASE WE HAVE TO RETREAT, AND A BIN TO HOLD OUR SNOW BALL RESERVES.

GOT IT.

HMM... THE SNOW DOESN'T PACK TOO WELL, DOES IT?

IT'S NOT WET ENOUGH.

GOSH, IT'LL TAKE FOREVER JUST TO BUILD THE OUTER WALL... EVEN WITHOUT THE TURRETS.

I'M COLD.

ME, TOO. LET'S GO IN.

MAYBE WE CAN HAVE SOME HOT CHOCOLATE BY A FIRE!

THIS IS MORE FUN THAN ACTUALLY BUILDING THE FORT ANYWAY. NOW WHERE SHOULD WE PUT THE ICICLE SPIKES?

ALL ALONG THE OUTER WALL, AFTER THE MOAT. ...SAY, I THINK YOU GOT MORE MARSHMALLOWS IN YOUR HOT CHOCOLATE THAN I DID.

THE BAY DOORS OPEN AND OUT FALLS CALVIN, THE C-BOMB!

CALVIN IS ABOUT TO UNLEASH THE PURE DESTRUCTIVE FORCE OF A MILLION A-BOMBS!

THE WORLD GASPS IN HORROR AS HE STREAKS TOWARD HIS TARGET!

OH NO YOU DON'T.!!

WILL YOU READ THIS TONIGHT?

"AN ODE TO TIGERS"?

HOBBES WROTE IT.

"THE ZEBRA'S STRIPES ARE LACKING HUES, SO THEY DON'T COMPARE TO YOU-KNOW-WHOSE."

"ORANGE, BLACK AND WHITE IS WHAT TO WEAR! IT'S HAUTE COUTURE FOR THOSE WHO DARE! IT'S CAMOUFLAGE, AND STYLISH, TOO! YES, TIGERS LOOK THE BEST, IT'S TRUE!"

THIS GOES ON?

FOR PAGES. PRETTY TEDIOUS, ISN'T IT?

I'M HO-OME!

KAPOW!

WUMPH!

GREAT. THE SNOW CUSHIONED THE BLOW TO MY SPINE, SO NOW I CAN DIE OF PNEUMONIA.

AWW, HAS OO GOT DE SNIFFOOS?

OK, LET'S SEE... IF THE WIND IS BLOWING NORTH-NORTHEAST AT 6 MPH, AND I THROW THE SNOWBALL DUE WEST AT 90 MPH WITH A SLIGHT TOP SPIN....

HA! SUSIE DIDN'T EVEN HEAR ME SNEAK UP!

NOW I'LL CREAM HER CRANIUM WITH A BARRAGE OF SNOWBALLS!

WHIZZZ

PIFF

PIFF

THESE DARN CROSS BREEZES! SHE DIDN'T EVEN NOTICE!

YOU'RE THE WORST SHOT IN THE WORLD, CALVIN! IF IT WASN'T FOR GRAVITY, YOU PROBABLY COULDN'T EVEN HIT THE GROUND!

SMACK!

I DID IT! I DID IT! JUST WHEN IT REALLY COUNTED, I *DID* IT! HA HA HA! RIGHT IN THE KISSER! HA HA!

BAD NEWS, MOM. I PROMISED MY SOUL TO THE DEVIL THIS AFTERNOON.

OH? THAT RECENTLY?

THE FEARLESS SPACEMAN SPIFF FINDS HIMSELF ON THE PLANET CLOSEST TO STAR X-351!

AN ALIEN APPROACHES... BUT IN THE BLINDING LIGHT, OUR HERO CAN HARDLY MAKE IT OUT! IS IT FRIENDLY OR HOSTILE?

WHAT ARE YOU DOING IN BED STILL?! GET READY FOR SCHOOL!

DEFINITELY HOSTILE.

THE SCHOOL BUS WILL BE HERE ANY MINUTE! GO! SCOOT!

SPACEMAN SPIFF, CAPTURED BY VICIOUS ZOGWARGS, IS ABOUT TO BE TRANSPORTED TO THE LABOR CAMP! OUR HERO HATCHES A BOLD PLAN!

AT THE LAST SECOND, SPIFF MAKES HIS BREAK! TAKING ADVANTAGE OF THE PLANET'S WEAKER GRAVITY, OUR HERO IS AWAY LIKE A SHOT.

THERE'S THE BUS... BUT WHY DON'T I SEE CALVIN?

SPIFF ESCAPES!

DID CALVIN GET ON THE BUS?

I DIDN'T SEE. ...WHY?

SOMEONE JUST DARTED BEHIND THAT TREE. SEE, THERE HE GOES AGAIN! ISN'T THAT CALVIN?

THE ZOGWARGS HAVE SPOTTED HIM! OUR HERO INFLATES THE EMERGENCY JET PACK HE KEEPS IN HIS POCKET, AND PREPARES FOR TAKEOFF!

CALVIN, WHAT ARE YOU DOING? YOU'RE SUPPOSED TO BE ON THE SCHOOL BUS! GET OVER HERE!

OUR HERO BLASTS OFF WITH HIS EMERGENCY JET PACK! ANOTHER DARING ESCAPE FOR THE INTREPID SPACEMAN SPIFF!

ZOUNDS! THE ZOGWARGS ARE ON ROCKET SCOOTERS! SPIFF FIRES HIS DEATH RAY BLASTER!

IT'S YOUR OWN GRAVE YOU'RE DIGGING, BUSTER!

YOUNG MAN, YOU ARE IN *VERY* BIG TROUBLE!

WHY DIDN'T YOU GET ON THE SCHOOL BUS?! NOW *I'VE* GOT TO DRIVE YOU, AND YOUR DAD WILL BE LATE FOR WORK!

YOU'VE INCONVENIENCED EVERYONE! WHAT HAVE YOU GOT TO SAY FOR YOURSELF?!

GIVE ME LIBERTY OR GIVE ME DEATH, ZOGWARG QUEEN!

DON'T TEMPT ME! AND LISTEN, YOU CALL ME *"MOM,"* ...*GOT* IT?

HEY, CALVIN, HOW COME YOU'RE LATE TODAY? WHY DIDN'T YOU RIDE THE BUS?

I WAS GOING TO SKIP SCHOOL, BUT I GOT CAUGHT.

REALLY? HOW?

MOM HAD THE WIND FOR THAT FINAL SPRINT.

YOUR MOM HAD TO *CHASE* YOU?

I COULDN'T BELIEVE IT WHEN SHE CLEARED THE HEDGE.

YES, CAN I HAVE THE TOOL DEPARTMENT, PLEASE? THANK YOU.

HELLO? HOW MUCH ARE YOUR POWER CIRCULAR SAWS? I SEE. AND YOUR ELECTRIC DRILLS? UH-HUH. HOW BIG OF A BIT WILL THAT HOLD? REALLY? GREAT.

SO THE ASSIGNMENT IS PAGES TWO THROUGH FOUR? OK, THANKS SUSIE.

..SORRY ABOUT THAT. DO YOU CARRY ACETYLENE TORCHES? OK, RING IT ALL UP. THIS WILL BE ON MASTERCARD.

LOOK AT ALL THIS HOMEWORK I'M SUPPOSED TO DO!

I DON'T WANT TO DO THIS GARBAGE! I WANT TO GO PLAY OUTSIDE!

CHILDHOOD IS SHORT AND MATURITY IS FOREVER.

PEOPLE ARE ROTTEN.

WHEN I GROW UP, I'M GOING TO LIVE A MILLION MILES AWAY FROM EVERYONE!

HOW WILL YOU SURVIVE? WHAT WILL YOU EAT?

...WELL, MOM COULD COME BY TWICE A DAY TO COOK, I SUPPOSE.

THAT WOULD BE QUITE A COMMUTE.

GET A LOAD OF *THIS* DUMB ASSIGNMENT! I'M SUPPOSED TO WRITE ABOUT AN ADVENTURE I'VE HAD!

I HAVEN'T HAD ANY ADVENTURES! MY LIFE HAS BEEN ONE BIG BORE FROM THE BEGINNING!

HAVE I EVER BEEN ABDUCTED BY PIRATES? HAVE I EVER FACED DOWN A CHARGING RHINO? HAVE I EVER BEEN IN A SHOOT-OUT, OR ON A BOMBING RAID? **NO!** I NEVER GET TO HAVE ADVENTURES!

WHAT ABOUT THE TIME YOU BACKED THE CAR THROUGH THE GARAGE DOOR?

YOU CALL THAT AN ADVENTURE? I DIDN'T EVEN GET ON THE HIGHWAY.

WHEN DO YOU THINK WE'LL GET A THUNDER AND LIGHTNING STORM?

I DON'T KNOW. PROBABLY NOT UNTIL SPRING.

I THINK HE'S GOING TO MELT BEFORE WE CAN BRING HIM TO LIFE.

HEY, SUSIE, STAND ON THIS "X."

WHY?

NO REASON. JUST DO IT. I DARE YOU.

NO.

PLEASE? C'MON!

GET LOST.

THIS MAY NOT WORK OUT AS WELL AS I THOUGHT.

WOW, YOU'VE MADE A LOT OF SNOWMEN TODAY!

YEP. THEY'RE EFFIGIES. EACH ONE REPRESENTS SOMEONE I HATE.

WHEN THE SUN COMES OUT, I'LL WATCH THEIR FEATURES SLOWLY MELT DOWN THEIR DRIPPING BODIES UNTIL THEY'RE NOTHING BUT NOSES AND EYES FLOATING IN POOLS OF WATER.

I WASN'T AWARE YOU EVEN KNEW THIS MANY PEOPLE.

THE ONES I *REALLY* HATE ARE SMALL, SO THEY'LL GO FASTER.

I'M WRITING A BOOK ABOUT MY LIFE.

IT'S CALLED, "CALVIN: THE SHOCKING TRUE STORY OF THE BOY WHOSE EXPLOITS PANICKED A NATION."

INTERESTING TITLE.

THANKS.

SPECIFICALLY WHAT EXPLOITS ARE YOU REFERRING TO?

THAT'S THE PROBLEM. CAN YOU HELP ME THINK OF SOME I COULD DO?

HI, SUSIE.

GO AWAY, CALVIN! SIT SOMEWHERE ELSE! I DON'T WANT TO KNOW WHAT REVOLTING THING YOU HAVE FOR LUNCH TODAY.

RELAX, SUSIE. I'M NOT GOING TO TELL YOU WHAT I HAVE.

YOU'D BETTER NOT. I MEAN IT.

ALL I'LL SAY IS THAT I SURE FEEL SORRY FOR MY TAPEWORM.

MISS WORMWOOD!

HEY! DID I *SAY* WHAT MY LUNCH IS?! *DID* I ?!?

CALVIN and HOBBES

by WATTERSON

WHAT'S THIS?

A CRASH TEST DUMMY. NOW I CAN SEE IF THE HILL IS SAFE TO GO DOWN.

OFF YOU GO!

OOH, I THINK I'M GOING TO BE SICK.

WELL I WOULDN'T HAVE STEERED LIKE *THAT!* HE DESERVED IT!

OH, NO! THE AIR PRESSURE IN THIS ROOM IS TOO HIGH!

CALVIN'S ORGANS ARE IN DANGER OF COLLAPSING! HE...HE'S ABOUT TO IMPLODE!

WE'VE GOT TO GET OUT OF HERE! THERE'S TOO MUCH ATMOSPHERE!

SIT STILL AND BEHAVE. WE CAN'T EAT AT FAST FOOD PLACES ALL THE TIME.

THESE TELEVISION PROGRAMS SURE ARE ROTTEN.

THERE ISN'T AN OUNCE OF IMAGINATION IN THE WHOLE BUNCH. WHAT BILGE.

WHO DO THEY THINK IS STUPID ENOUGH TO SIT AND WATCH THIS TRASH?

YOU.

IF THERE WAS ANYTHING *BETTER* ON, I'D WATCH *THAT.*

YOU'RE TAKING A SHOWER *NOW*? THAT MEANS YOU'RE GOING OUT TONIGHT, RIGHT?

AND YOU HAVEN'T TOLD *ME* TO GET CLEANED UP, SO THAT MEANS I'M STAYING HOME, RIGHT?

AND IF I'M STAYING HOME, THAT MEANS YOU'VE GOTTEN ME A BABY SITTER, RIGHT? AND THAT MEANS YOU'VE PROBABLY HIRED *ROSALYN*, RIGHT?!?

BRILLIANT, HOLMES.

AAHH HAHH!

QUICK, HOBBES! WE'VE GOT TO HIDE! MOM AND DAD GOT *ROSALYN* FOR OUR BABY SITTER AGAIN! AND YOU KNOW WHAT *THAT* MEANS!

IT USUALLY MEANS WE'RE IN BED BY 6:30.

RIGHT! NO TV, NO HORSING AROUND, *NOTHING*! SHE JUST WALKS IN AND SENDS US STRAIGHT TO BED!

AND THEN SHE DOESN'T EVEN KISS US GOOD NIGHT.

EWW, GROSS! YOU *WANT* HER TO?!?

WHERE ARE YOU GOING TONIGHT? WHY CAN'T HOBBES AND I COME? WHY DO WE HAVE TO HAVE A BABY SITTER?

WE'RE GOING TO DINNER AND A MOVIE JUST TO HAVE SOME TIME TO OURSELVES, OK?

BUT WE COULD COME! HOBBES PROMISES NOT TO KILL ANYONE! WE'D BE GOOD! REALLY! WHY WON'T YOU LET US COME? WHY DON'T YOU WANT US AROUND?

IS THE MOVIE DIRTY? WHAT'S THE PROBLEM?!

GOSH, A DINNER WITH REAL PAUSES IN THE CONVERSATION! CAN YOU IMAGINE?

HI, ROSALYN. COME ON IN. CALVIN'S UPSTAIRS HIDING FROM YOU, SO YOU MAY HAVE AN EASY EVENING.

THAT WOULD BE GREAT. I'VE GOT TO STUDY TONIGHT FOR A BIG TEST TOMORROW.

DID YOU HEAR *THAT*? DID YOU HEAR *THAT*?

HEE HEE!

TONIGHT: THE REVENGE OF THE BABY-SAT!

HI, ROSALYN! HOW ARE YOU? WHAT ARE YOU DOING? HOME-WORK?

RIGHT. I'VE GOT TO STUDY FOR AN EXAM TOMORROW, SO I WANT IT QUIET TONIGHT. GOT IT?

OH, YOU BET, ROZ. HOBBES AND I WON'T MAKE A PEEP. CAN I SEE WHAT YOU'RE STUDYING?

DON'T TOUCH ANYTH...

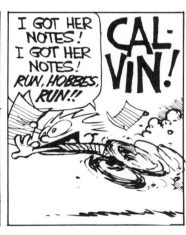

I GOT HER NOTES! I GOT HER NOTES! *RUN, HOBBES, RUN!!*

CAL-VIN!

GIVE ME BACK MY NOTES, YOU LITTLE CREEP!

RUN! RUN!

WHAT ARE WE GOING TO DO? SHE'LL KILL US!

INTO THE BATHROOM!

LOCK THE DOOR! QUICK!

CALVIN!

CLICK

OPEN THIS DOOR, OR YOUR PARENTS WILL NEVER FIND YOUR REMAINS!

BOY, SOME BABY SITTER!

HERE GO YOUR NOTES!

Calvin and Hobbes by Watterson

WHAT'S THIS?

A CALVIN DECOY. PRETTY GOOD, HUH?

NOW I CAN FIND OUT WHO MY ENEMIES ARE! I'LL HIDE BEHIND THAT TREE OVER THERE AND WATCH TO SEE WHO THROWS SNOWBALLS AT THE DECOY, THINKING IT'S ME!

YOUR ENEMIES MUST NOT BE VERY BRIGHT.

THAT'S WHY THEY'RE OUT TO GET ME. THEY CAN'T STAND MY GENIUS.

HEY, CALVIN! I SEE A WAY YOUR PLAN MIGHT FAIL.

PIPE DOWN, WILL YA? HOW CAN I HIDE WHEN YOU'RE YELLING TO ME FROM ACROSS...

SMACK!

SEE THERE? MY PLAN TO DISCOVER MY ENEMIES WAS A COMPLETE SUCCESS.

TOO BAD YOU TOOK OFF YOUR COAT AND HAT. YOU MUST BE SOAKED.

HERE WE ARE, POISED ON THE PRECIPICE OF "SUICIDE SLOPE." BELOW US LIE THE SKELETAL REMAINS OF HUNDREDS OF LITTLE SLED RIDERS.

SEARCHING FOR THAT ULTIMATE ADRENALINE RUSH, WE PREPARE TO HURL OURSELVES OVER THE BRINK! WHAT FATE AWAITS US?

READY?

NO.

LIFE AND DEATH HANG IN THE BALANCE! A FRACTION OF A SECOND AND ONE WRONG TURN ARE ALL THAT SEPARATE THEM!

THIS ISN'T HELPING.

DAD SAYS THE ANTICIPATION OF HAVING SOMETHING IS OFTEN MORE FUN THAN ACTUALLY HAVING IT.

I THINK HE'S CRAZY. I HATE WAITING FOR THINGS. I LIKE TO HAVE EVERYTHING IMMEDIATELY.

I CAN'T THINK OF *ANY*THING I'D RATHER ANTICIPATE THAN HAVE RIGHT AWAY. CAN YOU?

DEATH COMES TO MIND.

I DON'T KNOW WHY I BOTHER TRYING TO HAVE A LITTLE DISCUSSION WITH YOU WHEN YOU'RE ALWAYS SO MORBID.

I WISH SNOW WAS DRY, SO THAT YOU DIDN'T GET ALL COLD AND WET WHEN YOU PLAYED IN IT.

...THEN AGAIN, IF SNOW WAS DRY, YOU COULDN'T PACK IT INTO SNOWBALLS. THAT WOULDN'T BE GOOD.

I WISH IT SNOWED IN SUMMER. WOULDN'T THAT BE FUN? ...WELL NO, ACTUALLY THAT WOULD MAKE IT HARD TO RUN WHEN YOU PLAY BASEBALL.

HECK, IT'S OK JUST THE WAY IT IS.

WE'RE GLAD YOU APPROVE.

CALViN and HOBBES by WATTERSON

CLUMP

THE PTERANODON SPREADS HIS GIANT WINGS, AND..

Calvin and Hobbes by WATTERSON

I CAN NEVER ENJOY SUNDAYS, BECAUSE IN THE BACK OF MY MIND I ALWAYS KNOW I'VE GOT TO GO TO SCHOOL THE NEXT DAY.

IT'S LIKE TRYING TO ENJOY YOUR LAST MEAL BEFORE THE EXECUTION.

A PENNY FOR YOUR THOUGHTS.

SORRY. *MY* THOUGHTS ARE A BUCK APIECE.

A DOLLAR?! THAT'S OUTRAGEOUS! YOUR THOUGHTS AREN'T WORTH THAT!

THIS ONE IS! AT A DOLLAR, IT'S THE BARGAIN OF A LIFETIME.

I WOULDN'T PAY A NICKEL FOR ANY THOUGHT YOU'VE EVER HAD IN YOUR WHOLE FLEA-RIDDEN EXISTENCE!

THAT LITTLE REMARK JUST MADE THE PRICE *TEN* DOLLARS!

TEN?? YOU CAN'T EXTORT ME! *KEEP* YOUR STUPID THOUGHT!

IF YOU KNEW WHAT IT WAS, YOU'D *BEG* TO PAY TEN BUCKS FOR IT.

C'MON, JUST TELL ME WHAT IT IS, WILL YOU?

NOTHING DOING, PAL.

OK, OK! I'LL GIVE YOU 25 CENTS. THAT'S ALL I HAVE.

LET'S SEE IT.

HERE! 25 CENTS! NOW WHAT'S THIS BIG, EXPENSIVE THOUGHT OF YOURS?!

"A FOOL AND HIS MONEY ARE SOON PAR..."

48

LOOK AT THIS, HOBBES! I COULD ORDER AN OFFICIAL CHOCOLATE FROSTED SUGAR BOMBS BEANIE!

SEE, IT HAS A BATTERY-POWERED PROPELLER ON TOP AND A BIG STAR ON THE FRONT! ISN'T THAT NEAT?

YOU HAVE TO SEND IN FOUR BOX "PROOF OF PURCHASE SEALS" TO GET IT, IT SAYS.

WELL, DON'T JUST STAND THERE, OR THIS'LL TAKE FOREVER.

UGH. THIS STUFF ALWAYS MAKES MY HEART SKIP.

BLECHH. I FEEL SICK.

OH, C'MON, THAT'S ONLY YOUR SECOND BOWL OF CEREAL.

THIS STUFF IS PURE SUGAR.

BUT IT'S *FORTIFIED* WITH EIGHT ESSENTIAL VITAMINS, SO IT'S GOOD FOR YOU.

GIVE ME A BREAK. THIS IS LIKE EATING A BOWL OF MILK DUDS.

LOOK, IT SAYS RIGHT ON THE BOX, "PART OF A WHOLESOME, NUTRITIOUS, BALANCED BREAKFAST."

AND THEY SHOW A GUY EATING FIVE GRAPEFRUITS, A DOZEN BRAN MUFFINS...

YOU KNOW WHY YOU SHAKE LIKE THAT? VITAMIN DEFICIENCY, I'LL BET.

'MORNING, DAD! HOW'S YOUR BREAKFAST?

FINE.

OATMEAL, HUH? A BOWL OF PASTY, BLAND, COLORLESS SLUDGE.

YES. WHY DON'T YOU GO DESCRIBE YOUR *OWN* FOOD SOMEWHERE ELSE?

I'LL BET YOU'D RATHER HAVE A BOWL OF TASTY, LIP-SMACKING, CRUNCHY-ON-THE-OUTSIDE, CHEWY-ON-THE-INSIDE, CHOCOLATE FROSTED SUGAR BOMBS! CAN I POUR YOU SOME?

NO, THANKS. I'M TRYING TO REACH MIDDLE AGE.

WHAT ARE *YOU* HAVING, MOM? BORING OLD TOAST AND TEA?

YOU WANT THE BEANIE, *YOU* EAT THE CEREAL, CALVIN.

1½ BOXES TO GO, AND I'LL HAVE ENOUGH "PROOF OF PURCHASE SEALS" TO ORDER THE PROPELLER BEANIE THEY OFFER.

1⅓ BOXES TO GO.

MAN, I'M *EARNING* THIS.

HOBBES, I DID IT! I ATE ENOUGH BOXES OF CEREAL TO GET ALL THE PROOF OF PURCHASE SEALS I NEED!

NOW I CAN ORDER MY BEANIE! OH, BOY! I CAN'T WAIT TO GET IT! I'LL BE SO COOL!

NOT FOR OVER A MONTH. IT SAYS TO ALLOW SIX WEEKS FOR DELIVERY.

SIX WEEKS ?!? ...

I'LL BE *OLD* THEN!

AND I'M SURE YOUR BEANIE WILL BE THE TALK OF THE REST HOME.

SCHOOL

MOM! MOM! DID MY BEANIE COME IN THE MAIL?

ARE YOU KIDDING? I JUST MAILED YOUR ORDER THIS MORNING.

I'M NEVER GOING TO MAKE IT SIX WEEKS.

I CAN'T BELIEVE THIS. EVERY DAY I GET ALL MY HOPES UP, THINKING MY BEANIE WILL COME... AND THEN IT DOESN'T.

AND FOR EACH DAY THAT GOES BY, I FIGURE THE ODDS ARE BETTER THAT IT WILL COME THE *NEXT* DAY, SO MY HOPES GET HIGHER AND HIGHER BEFORE THEY FALL. IT'S AWFUL.

BUT I'VE BEEN DISAPPOINTED SO OFTEN NOW, I'M FINALLY GETTING NUMB TO IT.

MAYBE THE MAILMAN MADE A SECOND TRIP TODAY AND DELIVERED IT IN THE LAST FIVE MINUTES.

WOW! I NEVER THOUGHT OF THAT! C'MON!

HE'S NOT NUMB.

THE LONGER YOU WAIT FOR THE MAIL, THE LESS THERE IS IN IT.

I'M HOME. I DIDN'T GET MY PROPELLER BEANIE TODAY, DID I?

AS A MATTER OF FACT, YOU DID!

IT'S HERE!

HA HA! IT TOOK WEEKS AND WEEKS OF WAITING, BUT AT LONG LAST IT'S HERE! NOW I FINALLY, *FINALLY* GET TO PUT IT ON!

"SOME ASSEMBLY REQUIRED. BATTERIES NOT INCLUDED."

CAN YOU BELIEVE THIS? I'VE GOT TO ASSEMBLE MY BEANIE PROPELLER AND MOTOR MYSELF!

WHAT DO THEY THINK I AM, AN ENGINEER? LOOK, I'VE GOT TO INSERT THESE WIRES AND THIS PLASTIC SWITCH! I CAN'T DO THIS!

HERE, LET ME TRY.

NO! GET AWAY! *I'LL* DO IT! YOU'D PROBABLY GOOF IT ALL UP, OR...

* SNAP *

OH NO!

SEE? INSULT A TIGER AND YOU GET BAD LUCK! EVERY TIME!

MY MOTOR BROKE! THE PIECE SNAPPED! NOW MY BEANIE PROPELLER WON'T WORK!!

AAGHHGHHH! I WAITED *WEEKS* FOR THIS AND NOW IT'S *BROKEN*, AND I DIDN'T EVEN GET TO *WEAR* IT! STUPID ROTTEN PIECE OF LOUSY JUNK!!

IT'S ALL *YOUR* FAULT! RRGHH GHHGH!

MY FAULT?! I WAS JUST SITTING HERE! *YOU* BROKE IT!

YOU *WILLED* ME TO BREAK IT! YOU DID SOME SUBLIMINAL THING! DON'T DENY IT! I KNOW YOU DID! YOU *MUST* HAVE!

OK, *NOW* I'M WILLING YOU TO GO JUMP IN THE SEPTIC TANK.

WHAT ARE YOU MAD AT *ME* FOR?!

GET AWAY FROM ME! I DON'T EVEN WANT TO TALK TO YOU!

YOU BROKE YOUR BEANIE MOTOR, NOT *ME*! I DIDN'T DO ANYTHING!

YOU DISTRACTED ME!

I DID NOT! I WAS JUST *SITTING* HERE! YOU BROKE IT ALL BY YOURSELF!

* SNIFF * * SNIFFLE * ...ALL RIGHT.. I KNOW..

BUT CONSIDERING MY LIFE'S IN SHAMBLES RIGHT NOW, COULDN'T YOU AT LEAST TAKE THE BLAME?

C'MON, CALVIN! THIS IS THE THIRD TIME I'VE CALLED YOU. GET UP.

I DON'T WANT TO GET UP. I DON'T WANT TO GO TO SCHOOL.

WELL, YOU *HAVE* TO, WHETHER YOU WANT TO OR NOT, SO LET'S MOVE.

FOR YOUR INFORMATION, I DON'T *HAVE* TO DO ANYTHING I DON'T *WANT* TO DO.

IS THAT SO?

SHE SURE CAN MAKE SOMEONE WANT TO DO SOMETHING.

I DON'T WANT TO CATCH THE BUS. I DON'T WANT TO GO TO SCHOOL. I DON'T WANT TO BE HERE AT ALL.

I'M SICK OF EVERYONE TELLING ME WHAT TO DO ALL THE TIME! I HATE MY LIFE! I HATE EVERYTHING! I WISH I WAS *DEAD!*

... WELL, NO, I DON'T. NOT REALLY.

I WISH EVERYONE *ELSE* WAS DEAD.

HI, CALVIN.

HMPH.

OH, *YOU'RE* REAL PLEASANT THIS MORNING. WHAT'S THE MATTER WITH YOU?

GO STEP IN FRONT OF A CEMENT MIXER, OK?

WHAT A PILL YOU ARE! WHAT A JERK! WELL, WHO NEEDS *YOU?!* YOU CAN JUST STAND THERE AND BE GRUMPY ALL BY YOURSELF!

HMPH.

NOTHING HELPS A BAD MOOD LIKE SPREADING IT AROUND.

57

PHOOEY. NO BUGS IN THE BUS WINDOW.

I CAN'T BELIEVE YOU'RE DOING THIS.

CHOOL DISTRI

HEY, ASK THAT KID IF HE'S GOT ANY BUGS IN *HIS* WINDOW.

CALVIN, THERE IS NO WAY YOU'RE GOING TO COMPLETE AN INSECT COLLECTION ON THE WAY TO SCHOOL! FORGET IT!

SIGHHH... WELL, MAYBE YOU'RE RIGHT.

HOW MUCH DO YOU WANT FOR *YOUR* COLLECTION? I'LL GIVE YOU A QUARTER...OR HERE, 30 CENTS.

I SPENT A MONTH ON THIS!

HEY, HERE'S A WORM! WORMS ARE BUGS, AREN'T THEY?

EWW GROSS, CALVIN! THAT'S BEEN FLOATING IN A PUDDLE FOR DAYS.

CLASS DOESN'T START FOR 10 MINUTES. IF I CAN CATCH FIVE BUGS A MINUTE, I'LL GET AN "A" ON MY COLLECTION. SEE, I'M OFF TO A GOOD START.

FIVE BUGS A MINUTE?! YOU'RE OUT OF YOUR MIND.

HERE'S ANOTHER ALREADY.

THAT'S A LITTLE BALL OF LINT!

LIKE I'M SURE THE TEACHER'S GOING TO LOOK **REAL CLOSE** AT EVERY HAIRY BUG IN 30 KIDS' COLLECTIONS!

RINNGGGG

THERE'S THE BELL. WE'VE GOT TO GO TO CLASS.

RATS. I DIDN'T GET 50 BUGS YET.

WHAT DO YOU HAVE?

ONE DROWNED WORM, A PIECE OF FUZZY LINT THAT *LOOKS* LIKE A BUG, A LIVE ANT, AND A SMASHED FLY.

WELL, IF YOU LABEL THEM SCIENTIFICALLY IN THE NEXT 30 SECONDS, MAYBE YOU'LL GET AN "F+."

WE'VE GOT TO *LABEL* THESE *TOO*?!? I WAS JUST GOING TO PUT THEM ALL IN AN ENVELOPE.

ACTUALLY, I DON'T THINK THERE'S ANY WAY YOU'LL GET AN "F+."

FOR ALL THIS WORK, I'D BETTER AT LEAST GET A "D."

HERE COMES SUSIE, BACK FROM THE PRINCIPAL'S OFFICE. BOY, DOES SHE LOOK PALE. I WONDER WHAT HAPPENED. SHE'S TALKING TO THE TEACHER NOW.

PSST! SUSIE, WHAT DID THEY DO TO YOU? DID YOU GET EXPELLED? YOU DIDN'T SNITCH ON *ME*, DID YOU?

YOU *DID* SNITCH! YOU'RE A *STOOLIE!* A CANARY!

YOU'RE GOING UP THE RIVER, CALVIN.

CALVIN, WILL YOU COME HERE, PLEASE?

SO *FIRST* I GOT IN TROUBLE FOR NOT PAYING ATTENTION IN CLASS AND FOR TURNING IN A LAST-MINUTE INSECT COLLECTION, WHICH I GOT A "D-MINUS-MINUS" ON.

THEN I GOT IN TROUBLE FOR GETTING *SUSIE* IN TROUBLE WHEN I WANTED HER TO HELP ME FUDGE THE PROJECT.

THEN I GOT IN TROUBLE WHEN I TOLD MOM, AND *THEN* I GOT IN TROUBLE *AGAIN* WHEN *SHE* TOLD *DAD!* I'VE BEEN IN HOT WATER EVER SINCE I GOT UP!

WOW. I'LL BET ALL THIS MAKES YOU GET YOUR BOOK REPORT FINISHED RIGHT ON TIME.

MY WHAT?

ONE OF NATURE'S MOST PECULIAR-LOOKING CREATURES, THE GIRAFFE IS UNIQUELY SUITED TO ITS ENVIRONMENT.

HIS TREMENDOUS HEIGHT ENABLES HIM TO MUNCH ON THE SUCCULENT MORSELS MOST DIFFICULT TO REACH.

CALVIN and HOBBES

by WATTERSON

GOTCHA!!

!

HEY! JUST WHAT DO YOU THINK YOU'RE DOING BACK DOWN *HERE*?!

YOU DIDN'T READ ME MY RIGHTS.

DAD! DAD! OUTER SPACE ALIENS JUST LANDED IN THE BACK YARD!

OH, REALLY. WHAT DO THEY LOOK LIKE?

SORT OF LIKE BIG BAKED POTATOES WITH LASER GUNS. I THINK WE SHOULD DO WHAT THEY SAY.

DID THEY SAY WHAT THEY WANT?

YEAH, THEY WANT 10 DOLLARS.

I'LL BET THEY DO.

SINCE YOU'RE SO BUSY, YOU CAN JUST GIVE THE MONEY TO ME, AND I'LL TAKE IT OVER TO THEM.

HOW COME **YOU** ALWAYS READ ME MY BEDTIME STORY AND NOT MOM?

BECAUSE READING THE BEDTIME STORY IS THE *DAD'S* JOB.

AND IT APPEARS TO BE THE *ONLY* "DAD'S JOB" AROUND HERE!

LEFT THE DISHES FOR MOM AGAIN, HUH?

TONIGHT'S STORY IS CALLED, "WHY PRINCE CHARMING STAYED SINGLE."

PRINCE **WHAT**?

I'VE BEEN THINKING. SUPPOSE I GROW UP TO BE ONE OF THE WORLD'S GREATEST MEN OF ALL TIME. SUPPOSE MY NAME WILL BE AN INSPIRATION TO HUMANITY FOR EONS TO COME!

WHAT WILL THE HISTORY BOOKS SAY? THEY'LL SAY, "MUCH OF HIS CHILDHOOD WAS SPENT UNWILLINGLY IN THE BATHTUB."

WHAT AN INDIGNITY THIS BATH IS! IS THIS SITUATION WORTHY OF ONE OF THE GREATEST MEN OF ALL TIME ?!?

MY LIKELY HISTORICAL SIGNIFICANCE IS A TERRIBLE BURDEN.

WOULD YOU RATHER THEY SAID YOUR CHILDHOOD WAS DIRTY AND SMELLY?

NNNGKGKK

HOCCHHHH

PTOOEY!

BOY, THEY SURE GO FARTHER WHEN YOU MAKE 'EM RIGHT!

LET'S MAKE UP A *NEW* CONTEST, OK?

Calvin and Hobbes

by WATTERSON

THREE... TWO... ONE...

LIGHT SPEED!

BLASTING ACROSS THE GALAXY IN HYPER LIGHT DRIVE, IT'S *SPACEMAN SPIFF*, INTERPLANETARY EXPLORER EXTRAORDIN...

SINCE CALVIN SEEMS TO BE ENJOYING THE LESSON, LET'S HAVE HIM DEMONSTRATE THE NEXT PROBLEM.

ZOUNDS! A ZOK DEATH SLOOP APPEARS OUT OF NOWHERE AND FRIES SPIFF'S STABILIZERS!

OUR HERO HURLS OUT OF CONTROL TOWARD HIS IMMINENT DOOM!

THE SITUATION IS DESPERATE! THIS COULD BE THE END! WHAT CAN OUR HERO DO??

HIS MIND RACING FURIOUSLY, SPIFF SPRINGS INTO ACTION! HE DOWNSHIFTS HIS SPACECRAFT AND...

... STALLS.

RINGG!

OH, DARN, OUT OF TIME.

ONCE AGAIN SPACEMAN SPIFF BEATS ALL ODDS TO SAVE THE DAY!

HIC HIC HIC

(HIC) I HAVE (HIC) HAVE (HIC) I (HIC) I HAVE THE (HIC) THE (HIC)...

THE HIC (HIC) THE (HIC)

WHAT IS IT? WHAT DO YOU HAVE? A DOLLAR?? A NEW COMIC BOOK? WHAT??

THE (HIC HIC) I HAVE (HIC) HAVE THE (HIC) THE (HIC) THE HIC (HIC) THE (HIC)...

I LOVE DOING THIS.

HELP ME (HIC) GET (HIC) RID OF (HIC) THESE DARN (HIC) HIC (HIC) HICCUPS!

HOW?

(HIC) SCARE ME.

OK...

OUR OCEANS ARE FILLED WITH GARBAGE, WE'VE CREATED A HOLE IN THE OZONE THAT'S FRYING THE PLANET, NUCLEAR WASTE IS PILING UP WITHOUT ANY SAFE WAY TO GET RID OF IT ....

(HIC) I MEAN, *SURPRISE* ME (HIC).

THAT DOESN'T?! BOY, YOU'RE CYNICAL.

HERE. DRINKING FROM THE FAR SIDE OF A GLASS IS SUPPOSED TO CURE HICCUPS.

THE (HIC) FAR SIDE OF (HIC) THE GLASS? (HIC) HOW DO I (HIC) DO *THAT*?

YOU HAVE TO BEND YOUR HEAD WAY OVER.

OH (HIC) I SEE.

(HIC) THANKS. NOW I'VE GOT THE HICCUPS *AND* WATER UP MY NOSE.

I THINK MOST HICCUP CURES WERE REALLY INVENTED FOR THE AMUSEMENT OF THE PATIENT'S FRIENDS.

OH MY GOSH!! SOMEBODY BROKE INTO OUR HOUSE!!

I'LL CALL THE POLICE!

WHERE'S HOBBES?

I CAN'T BELIEVE THIS IS HAPPENING! LOOK AT THIS ROOM!

HOBBES! OH, I *KNEW* WE SHOULDN'T HAVE LEFT HIM HERE!

MOM, I CAN'T FIND HOBBES! HELP ME FIND HIM! WHAT IF... WHAT IF THEY...

IT'S OK, CALVIN. CALM DOWN. I'M SURE HOBBES IS HERE SOME-WHERE.

I DON'T THINK ANYONE WOULD STEAL A STUFFED TIGER. C'MON, LET'S GO LOOK.

BUT HOBBES IS SO *TRUSTING*..

SNIFF

THE POLICE SAY THEY'LL SEND SOMEONE OVER. HAVE YOU FIGURED OUT WHAT ALL IS MISSING?

NO, WE'RE LOOKING FOR HOBBES. CALVIN'S ALMOST HYSTERICAL.

I FEEL A LITTLE HYSTER-ICAL MYSELF.

OOH...I HOPE THE POLICE GET HERE QUICK. I'M SCARED.

THIS IS ONE OF THOSE THINGS YOU ALWAYS FIGURE WILL HAPPEN TO SOMEONE ELSE.

...UNFORTUNATELY, WE'RE *ALL* "SOMEONE ELSE" TO SOMEONE ELSE.

HOBBES? HOBBES? WHERE ARE YOU ??

I *TOLD* MOM AND DAD WE LEFT HOBBES BEHIND.... I *TRIED* TO GET THEM TO TURN AROUND AND COME BACK .... AND *NOW* LOOK, HOBBES WAS ALL ALONE WHEN OUR HOUSE WAS BROKEN INTO!

MOM SAYS HOBBES WOULDN'T HAVE BEEN STOLEN BECAUSE HE'S NOT VALUABLE.

...(SNIFF) WELL, *I* THINK HE'S VALUABLE.

HOBBES? ARE YOU DOWN HERE? YOU'VE GOT TO BE *SOME*WHERE!

HERE HE IS, CALVIN! I FOUND HOBBES!

YOU *FOUND* HIM! IS HE OK?? HE'S NOT HURT, IS HE?

HE'S FINE. HE WAS UNDER THE BED COVERS.

HOBBES, I'M SO GLAD TO SEE YOU!! YOU'RE SAFE AND SOUND! (SNIFF) AND NOW I AM, TOO!

IT LOOKS LIKE WE'RE A WHOLE FAMILY AGAIN.

SUCH AS IT IS, YES.

...AND THE TELEVISION'S GONE, TOO.

DO YOU HAPPEN TO HAVE THE SERIAL NUMBER?

I'LL BET THE BURGLARS GOT SCARED OFF WHEN THEY SAW THERE WAS A TIGER IN THE HOUSE! HOBBES WAS HERE THE WHOLE TIME!

CALVIN, NOT NOW, OK? I'M BUSY.

NOBODY STICKS AROUND LONG WHEN HE SEES A TIGER, THAT'S FOR SURE! MANDIBLES OF DEATH, THAT'S WHAT HOBBES HAS!

RIGHT. WHY DON'T YOU GO TELL YOUR MOM?

MAYBE HOBBES SHOULD LOOK AT SOME MUG SHOTS. CAN WE GO TO THE STATION AND IDENTIFY SUSPECTS? HUH, CAN WE?

DEAR!

I SURE MEET THE WEIRDOS IN THIS JOB...

I'VE SWEPT UP MOST OF THE GLASS FROM THE WINDOW.

OK, I'LL GET SOMETHING TO COVER UP THE HOLE.

DO YOU THINK IT'S SAFE TO STAY HERE TONIGHT? SUPPOSE THE BURGLARS COME BACK!

THE POLICE SAID THEY'D DRIVE BY, AND WE'LL LEAVE LOTS OF LIGHTS ON.

UGH, IT'S SO CREEPY KNOWING THESE GOONS HAVE BEEN IN OUR HOUSE. I DON'T FEEL SAFE AT ALL.

I KNOW. AND THIS MUST *REALLY* BE SCARY FOR A LITTLE KID LIKE CALVIN.

GOSH, I CAN'T WAIT TO TELL EVERYONE AT SCHOOL HOW OUR HOUSE GOT ROBBED!

BE SURE TO SAY WHO SCARED THE BURGLARS AWAY AFTER THEY TOOK THE TV AND JEWELRY.

IS CALVIN ASLEEP?

YES, HE'S SNUGGLED UP WITH HOBBES.

BOY, I DON'T KNOW HOW *I'M* EVER GOING TO SLEEP.

ME NEITHER. I CAN'T GET OVER WHAT'S HAPPENED.

THE IDEA OF SOME CRAZY STRANGER GOING THROUGH OUR HOUSE... *BRRRR!!* I WISH *I* HAD A BIG STUFFED ANIMAL TO FEEL SAFE WITH.

I GUESS YOU'LL HAVE TO DO.

SO WHAT DO *I* GET TO SNUGGLE? HOW COME *I'M* THE GROWN-UP??

THIS IS GOING TO BE A LONG NIGHT.

MY HEART JUMPS AT THE SLIGHTEST SOUND. IT'S ALMOST 2, AND I'M WIDE AWAKE.

WHEN SOMEONE BREAKS INTO YOUR HOME, IT SHATTERS YOUR LAST ILLUSION OF SECURITY. IF YOU'RE NOT SAFE IN YOUR OWN HOME, YOU'RE NOT SAFE ANYWHERE.

A MAN'S HOME IS HIS CASTLE, BUT IT SHOULDN'T HAVE TO BE A FORTRESS.

ARE YOU STILL AWAKE TOO?

MM-HMM. I WAS THINKING.

IT'S FUNNY... WHEN I WAS A KID, I THOUGHT GROWN-UPS NEVER WORRIED ABOUT ANYTHING. I TRUSTED MY PARENTS TO TAKE CARE OF EVERYTHING, AND IT NEVER OCCURRED TO ME THAT THEY MIGHT NOT KNOW HOW.

I FIGURED THAT ONCE YOU GREW UP, YOU AUTOMATICALLY KNEW WHAT TO DO IN ANY GIVEN SCENARIO.

I DON'T THINK I'D HAVE BEEN IN SUCH A HURRY TO REACH ADULTHOOD IF I'D KNOWN THE WHOLE THING WAS GOING TO BE AD-LIBBED.

WELL, AT LEAST WE WEREN'T HOME WHEN OUR HOUSE WAS BROKEN INTO. NO ONE WAS HURT. WE'RE ALL TOGETHER AND OK.

WE LOST A FEW OF OUR NICE THINGS, BUT THINGS DON'T MATTER MUCH REALLY.

IT'S HARD TO BELIEVE HOW OFTEN WE FORGET THAT.

CAN I BE EXCUSED NOW?

YOU DIDN'T FINISH YOUR DINNER.

WELL, I DIDN'T LIKE IT VERY MUCH, AND THERE'S THIS TV SHOW I WANT TO WATCH, SO...

OUR TV WAS STOLEN, REMEMBER?

GOSH, I GUESS I'LL EAT MY ASPARAGUS, DO MY HOMEWORK, AND GO STRAIGHT TO BED, THEN.

AND WE'RE SO PROUD OF HOW YOU HANDLE ADVERSITY.

THIS IS WHERE OUR TELEVISION USED TO BE.

BUT WE DON'T HAVE A TV ANYMORE. NOW WE HAVE A BLANK WALL TO WATCH.

SO HERE I AM, NOT BEING ENTERTAINED.

A POINTLESS EXISTENCE, HUH?

I MEAN, THE WALL IS EVEN PLAIN OLD *WHITE!*

CaLviN and HobbEs

by WATTERSON

I CAN'T SLEEP.

I THINK NIGHTTIME IS DARK SO YOU CAN IMAGINE YOUR FEARS WITH LESS DISTRACTION.

AT NIGHTTIME, THE WORLD ALWAYS SEEMS SO BIG AND SCARY, AND I ALWAYS SEEM SO SMALL.

I WISH I COULD FALL ASLEEP, SO IT WOULD BE MORNING.

SIGHHHHH..

LOOK AT HOBBES. HE'S ASLEEP.

Z

HEH HEH... HE SURE LOOKS FUNNY WHEN HE SLEEPS. TIGERS CLOSE THEIR EYES SO TIGHT. I WONDER WHAT HE'S DREAMING ABOUT.

GOOD OL' HOBBES. WHAT A FRIEND.

Z

THINGS ARE NEVER QUITE AS SCARY WHEN YOU'VE GOT A BEST FRIEND.

Z

Z

Z   Z

HI, CALVIN! WHAT ARE YOU DOING, MAKING PAPER HATS? CAN I MAKE ONE, TOO?

DON'T BE RIDICULOUS. THIS IS THE OFFICIAL CHAPEAU OF OUR TOP-SECRET CLUB, G.R.O.S.S. — GET RID OF SLIMY GIRLS!

"SLIMY GIRLS"?!

I KNOW THAT'S REDUNDANT, BUT OTHERWISE IT DOESN'T SPELL ANYTHING. NOW GO AWAY.

GIRLS AREN'T SLIMY!

DON'T GET GUNK ON ME. I TOOK A BATH LAST SATURDAY AND I'M ALL CLEAN.

I CAN'T BELIEVE YOU STARTED A SECRET CLUB JUST TO EXCLUDE GIRLS! THERE'S NOTHING WRONG WITH GIRLS!

SEE, HOBBES? GIRLS ARE SO EMOTIONAL.

YOU'RE THE MEANEST, MOST ROTTEN LITTLE KID I KNOW! WELL, FINE! PLAY WITH YOUR STUFFED TIGER! SEE WHAT I CARE! I DON'T WANT TO PLAY WITH A STINKER LIKE YOU ANYWAY!!

WOW, WHAT A GREAT CLUB!

OK, WE'VE GOT A SIGN FOR OUR SECRET CLUB, SO NOW WE NEED TO FIND A SECRET MEETING PLACE.

I KNOW! WE CAN SET UP A CARD TABLE IN THE GARAGE! THAT WOULD BE PERFECT FOR DRAWING UP MAPS AND STUFF!

HMM, THERE'S NOT MUCH ROOM WITH THE CAR HERE. LET'S PUSH IT INTO THE DRIVE.

SHOULDN'T YOU ASK YOUR MOM TO MOVE IT INSTEAD?

NAHH. SHE WON'T CARE IF WE PUSH IT OUT. C'MON.

IN THE PAST, YOU'VE BEEN A REMARKABLY POOR JUDGE OF WHAT YOUR MOM CARES ABOUT.

True friends are hard to come by.

I need more money.

I wish people were more like animals.

Animals don't try to change you or make you fit in. They just enjoy the pleasure of your company.

Animals aren't conditional about friendships. Animals like you just the way you are.

They listen to your problems, they comfort you when you're sad, and all they ask in return is a little kindness.

WHOOONK!
SOB IT'S SO...SO TRUE!
HOOOOT!
THBPBTPTH!

...AND SPEAKING OF "A LITTLE KINDNESS," I'D HAVE A TUNA FISH SANDWICH ANY TIME SOON THAT YOU HAPPEN TO MAKE ONE...

OF COURSE, SOME ANIMALS GET ON YOUR NERVES ONCE IN A WHILE.

HERE'S THE LATEST POLL OF HOUSEHOLD 6-YEAR-OLDS, DAD.

AN OVERWHELMING MAJORITY EXPRESS AMAZEMENT AT HOW LITTLE YOU'VE ACCOMPLISHED AS DAD SO FAR. THE IMPRESSION IS THAT YOU'RE AVOIDING ALL THE HARD DECISIONS THAT NEED TO BE MADE.

IN FACT, NONE OF THOSE POLLED COULD NAME A SINGLE INSTANCE OF TRUE PATERNAL LEADERSHIP.

HOW ABOUT IF I LEAD YOU UPSTAIRS TO YOUR BED?

HA HA. IF WE CAN BE SERIOUS FOR A MOMENT, I HAVE SOME INNOVATIVE IDEAS ABOUT MY ALLOWANCE.

LOOK AT ALL THESE ANTS.

THEY'RE ALL RUNNING LIKE MAD, WORKING TIRELESSLY ALL DAY, NEVER STOPPING, NEVER RESTING.

AND FOR WHAT? TO BUILD A TINY LITTLE HILL OF SAND THAT COULD BE WIPED OUT AT ANY MOMENT.' ALL THEIR WORK COULD BE FOR NOTHING, AND YET THEY KEEP ON BUILDING. THEY NEVER GIVE UP!

I SUPPOSE THERE'S A LESSON IN THAT.

YEAH ... ANTS ARE MORONS. LET'S SEE WHAT'S ON TV.

BOY, WHAT A GROUCH.

CALVIN and HOBBES

by WATTERSON

MILD-MANNERED CALVIN IS STUCK INSIDE DOING MATH PROBLEMS ON A BEAUTIFUL SUNDAY.

NO ONE IS WATCHING! HE DASHES INTO HIS CLOSET! *THIS* IS A JOB FOR...

STUPENDOUS MAN!

DEFENDER OF FREEDOM! ADVOCATE OF LIBERTY!

A BRIGHT CRIMSON STREAK BLASTS UP THROUGH THE ATMOSPHERE, AND THEN TURNS BACK TOWARD EARTH!

GAINING STUPENDOUS MOMENTUM, *STUPENDOUS MAN* STRIKES THE GROUND AT AN ACUTE ANGLE WITH STUPENDOUS FORCE!

THE EARTH SLOWLY STOPS ROTATING... AND BEGINS TO TURN IN THE OPPOSITE DIRECTION!

PUSHING WITH ALL HIS MIGHT, *STUPENDOUS MAN* TURNS THE PLANET ALL THE WAY AROUND BACKWARD! THE SUN SETS IN THE EAST AND RISES IN THE WEST! SOON IT'S 10 A.M. THE PREVIOUS DAY!

WHAT ARE YOU DOING OUTSIDE? DID YOU FINISH YOUR HOMEWORK ALREADY?

IT'S SATURDAY! I DON'T NEED TO DO IT UNTIL TOMORROW... THANKS TO *STUPENDOUS MAN!*

WHERE ARE *YOU* GOING?

OUT.

DID YOU PICK UP YOUR ROOM LIKE I ASKED YOU TO?

NO.

SO WHEN YOU SAY YOU'RE GOING "OUT," YOU REALLY MEAN YOU'RE GOING BACK UPSTAIRS TO CLEAN YOUR ROOM, RIGHT?

ENGLISH MUST NOT BE HER FIRST LANGUAGE.

WHAT ARE YOU DOING DOWN HERE AGAIN? DIDN'T I JUST SEND YOU TO CLEAN YOUR ROOM?!

TWISTED FIEND! NO FOUR WALLS CAN HOLD **STUPENDOUS MAN!** YOU'VE BEEN FOILED AGAIN, EVIL MOM-LADY! HA HA HA!

OH YEAH?

GREAT ZOK! SHE'S FIXED HER MIND-SCRAMBLING EYEBALL RAY ON ME! I'M SUDDENLY FILLED WITH THE DESIRE TO GO BACK UPSTAIRS AND DO HER NEFARIOUS BIDDING!

GLAD TO HEAR IT.

"CLEAN UP YOUR ROOM! CLEAN UP YOUR ROOM!" THAT'S ALL I EVER HEAR!

IT'S *MY* ROOM, RIGHT?!? IF *I* DON'T MIND THE MESS, WHAT BUSINESS IS IT OF ANYONE ELSE?! THIS IS TYRANNY! I *HATE* CLEANING MY ROOM!

IT'S GOING TO TAKE ME ALL *DAY* TO DO THIS! OOH, THIS MAKES ME MAD! A WHOLE DAY SHOT! WASTED! DOWN THE DRAIN! GONE!

AARGH!

ARE YOU KIDDING? HOW COULD THIS POSSIBLY TAKE ALL DAY?

HECK, IT'LL BE ANOTHER HOUR BEFORE I'M EVEN THROUGH GRIPING.

LET'S FACE IT, WE'RE AESTHETES.

HERE COMES SUSIE. JUST IGNORE HER.

HI, CALVIN. CAN I PLAY WITH YOU AND YOUR TIGER?

HOBBES AND I ARE *NOT* PLAYING. WE'RE DOING BIG IMPORTANT THINGS, AND WE DON'T NEED YOU TO MESS THEM UP.

IT DOESN'T LOOK TO *ME* LIKE YOU'RE DOING ANYTHING SO IMPORTANT.

WELL WE ARE, SO GO AWAY. WE'VE WASTED TOO MUCH TIME TALKING TO YOU ALREADY.

YOU'RE JUST PLAYING IN THE MUD!

THAT'S JUST WHAT IT *LOOKS* LIKE TO IGNORANT GIRLS LIKE YOU! GET LOST!

ALL RIGHT, YOU LITTLE CREEP! I DON'T NEED YOU! I'VE GOT BETTER THINGS TO DO THAN SIT IN THE MUD LIKE A PIG!

A PIG?! BY GOLLY, I'LL SHOW *YOU!*

DON'T BEND OVER! YOUR CURLY PINK TAIL SHOWS! OINK! OINK! OINK! OINK!

EAT SOME MUD, SUSIE!

HA HA! YOU MISSED! OINK! OINK! OINK!

AHHH, SPRING! THAT MAGICAL TIME OF YEAR WHEN A YOUNG MAN'S FANCY TURNS TO LOVE!

SHUT UP.

HELP! A BEE! A BEE! RUN FOR YOUR LIFE!

HOBBES! DID YOU SEE IT?? IT WAS THE BIGGEST BEE IN THE WORLD! IT WAS THE SIZE OF A KAISER ROLL! IT MUST'VE WEIGHED 70 POUNDS!

IT SOUNDED LIKE A HELICOPTER, AND ITS STINGER WAS LIKE A HARPOON! IT MUST'VE BEEN A KILLER DEATH BEE! MAN, I'M LUCKY IT DIDN'T GET ME!

LIFE IN THE GREAT SUBURBAN OUTBACK IS CERTAINLY FRAUGHT WITH PERIL.

IF YOU'D SEEN IT, YOU'D HAVE BEEN SCARED, TOO.

I CAN'T IMAGINE MASTERING THE SKILLS INVOLVED HERE WITHOUT A CLEARER UNDERSTANDING OF WHO'S GOING TO BE IMPRESSED.

I SAW THE MAN IN THE MOON TONIGHT.

MM.

I DIDN'T KNOW THE MOON MADE FACES.

THAT'S "PHASES."

calvin and hobbes

by WATTERSON

AHHHH...

UH-OH. SOMETHING IS SERIOUSLY WRONG HERE.

THE LAWS OF PERSPECTIVE HAVE BEEN REPEALED!

OBJECTS NO LONGER DIMINISH IN SIZE WITH DISTANCE!

LINES DO NOT CONVERGE TOWARD ANY POINT ON THE HORIZON!

ALL SPATIAL RELATIONSHIPS ARE LOST! IT'S IMPOSSIBLE TO JUDGE WHERE ANY-THING IS! OH NO!

CALVIN, QUIT RUNNING AROUND AND CRASHING INTO THINGS, OR I'LL SELL YOU TO THE MONKEY HOUSE!

...AND NOW *SHE'S* LOST PERSPECTIVE.

THE GIANT PTERANODON HOPS TO THE EDGE OF THE CLIFF.

THERE HE SPREADS HIS BAT-LIKE WINGS AND TAKES TO THE AIR! SOARING HIGH OVER THE PREHISTORIC VALLEY, THE PTERANODON IS TRULY A MAJESTIC SIGHT!

THAT'S IT, THINK MAJESTIC!

I'M THINKING WE SHOULD'VE PICKED A SMALLER CLIFF!

IT'S TOO DARN HOT OUT HERE.

YOU COULD GO WADING IN THE CREEK.

THIS WATER IS TOO DARN COLD.

YOU COULD GO SIT IN THE SHADE THEN.

THIS SHADE IS TOO DARN DARK.

YOU COULD GO SIT IN YOUR ROOM WITH THE WINDOWS SHUT AND THE FAN AND LIGHTS ON.

THAT'S WHAT I WAS DOING WHEN MOM THREW ME OUT HERE.

I WAS KIDDING.

GIVE ME SOME COOKIES, OR I SOAK YOU WITH THIS WATER BALLOON!

WHY, YOU LITTLE THUG! DON'T YOU THREATEN YOUR MOTHER! AND DON'T EVEN *THINK* ABOUT THROWING THAT IN THE HOUSE!

OUT! OUT!

I'LL BET I'D HAVE GOTTEN SOME COOKIES IF I HAD FILLED THIS WITH *PAINT*.

AAUGH GRRRRRR

WHAM!

YOU CAN TAKE THE TIGER OUT OF THE JUNGLE, BUT YOU CAN'T TAKE THE JUNGLE OUT OF THE TIGER!

THE QUESTION *IS*, HOW CAN YOU GET THE TIGER *BACK* IN THE JUNGLE?

IT'S JULY ALREADY! OH NO! OH NO!

WHAT HAPPENED TO JUNE?! SUMMER VACATION IS SLIPPING THROUGH OUR FINGERS LIKE GRAINS OF SAND!

IT'S GOING TOO FAST! WE'VE GOT TO HOARD OUR FREEDOM AND HAVE MORE FUN! TIME RUSHES ON! HELP! HELP!

I DON'T THINK I WANT TO BE HERE AT THE END OF AUGUST.

AAUGH! IT'S A HALF-HOUR LATER THAN IT WAS HALF AN HOUR AGO! RUN! RUN!

MOM TOOK ME TO THE LIBRARY TODAY, DAD.

THAT'S NICE. DID YOU GET OUT A BOOK?

YEP. IT'S GREAT! I HAD NO IDEA BOOKS COULD BE SO MUCH FUN.

AND YOU'LL LEARN THINGS, TOO.

I'LL SAY! MY BOOK SAYS THAT THIS ONE WASP LAYS ITS EGG ON A SPIDER, SO WHEN THE EGG HATCHES, THE LARVA EATS THE SPIDER, SAVING THE VITAL ORGANS FOR LAST, SO THE SPIDER STAYS ALIVE WHILE IT'S BEING DEVOURED!

GROSS, HUH?

ISN'T THERE A STREET CORNER WHERE HE COULD HANG OUT INSTEAD?

AND COLOR PICTURES, TOO! WANT TO SEE 'EM?

I'M DESTINED FOR GREATNESS, I JUST KNOW IT. "CALVIN THE GREAT," THEY'LL CALL ME.

AND THINK HOW LUCKY *YOU'LL* BE! YOU'LL GET TO TELL EVERYONE HOW YOU KNEW ME AS A KID! WHAT A PRIVILEGE!

IN FACT, ALL THE PAPERS AND MAGAZINES WILL PROBABLY WANT TO INTERVIEW YOU TO FIND OUT WHAT I'M REALLY LIKE.

AND BOY, WILL YOU HAVE TO COUGH UP TO KEEP ME QUIET.

AND WHAT'S *THAT* SUPPOSED TO MEAN?!

DO RE MI FA
SO LA TI DO

A SPARROW ALIGHTS UPON A TREE BRANCH.

BUT THIS IS NO *ORDINARY* SPARROW! THIS IS A *SONG* SPARROW!

SWAYING GENTLY IN THE BREEZE, HE PREPARES TO BURST FORTH IN RAPTUROUS MELODY!

ON TOP OF SPA-GHETTI

ALL COVERED WITH CHEEEESE, I LOST MY POOR MEEEATBALLL, WHEN...

WUM WUM WUM

HOW'S IT GOING?

FINE. CLOSE THE LID. EVERYTHING STOPS WHEN YOU OPEN IT.

I WISH *MY* BATHTUB HAD AN AGITATOR.

CALVIN, WILL YOU GATHER THE TRASH, PLEASE?

GATHER THE TRASH?!? WHAT AM I, YOUR PERSONAL *SLAVE*?! WHY CAN'T *YOU* DO IT?

FINE, I WILL. AND *YOU* CAN START WASHING YOUR *OWN* CLOTHES, AND FIXING YOUR *OWN* MEALS, AND PICKING UP YOUR *OWN* TOYS, AND MAKING YOUR *OWN* BED, AND CLEANING UP YOUR *OWN* MESSES, DAY AFTER DAY AFTER *DAY!*

SOME WOMEN JUST WEREN'T MEANT TO BE MOTHERS.

WHENEVER I COOK AN EGG, I LIKE TO SEE HOW HIGH I CAN CRACK IT ABOVE THE SKILLET.

THEN I AIM WITH JUST ONE EYE OPEN, SO I DON'T HAVE ANY DEPTH PERCEPTION. IT'S PRETTY HARD THAT WAY.

SEE, THE SECRET TO HAVING FUN IN LIFE IS TO MAKE LITTLE CHALLENGES FOR YOURSELF.

CRIKK

LIKE THE CHALLENGE OF EXPLAINING THE STOVE AND FLOOR TO YOUR MOM?

RATS. SEE IF THERE'S ANOTHER CARTON IN THE FRIDGE, WILL YA?

CaLviN and HobbEs

by WATTERSON

CLICK

UH OH...

THE SKY IS A DEEP ORANGE! CALVIN'S SKIN IS A PALE GREEN! YELLOW FLOWERS ARE NOW BLUE!

EVERY COLOR IS THE OPPOSITE OF WHAT IT SHOULD BE!

CALVIN HAS BEEN TRANSFERRED TO A COLOR FILM NEGATIVE!

HIS ONLY HOPE IS TO BE PROCESSED BY A 1-HOUR PHOTO FINISHER! DEVELOPER! I NEED DEVELOPER!

DOGGONE IT, CALVIN! THAT'S ANOTHER PICTURE RUINED! CAN'T YOU LOOK PLEASANT FOR 1/500TH OF A SECOND?!

WHAT ARE YOU WRITING?

I'M TELLING THESE COMPANIES I INTEND TO BOYCOTT ALL THEIR PRODUCTS IF THEY DON'T PULL THEIR ADS FROM A TV SHOW I FIND OFFENSIVE.

BY GOLLY, IF THESE COMPANIES ARE GOING TO SUPPORT OBJECTIONABLE TV PROGRAMS, I'LL TAKE MY BUSINESS ELSEWHERE!

MAYBE I CAN SCARE AWAY THE ADVERTISING DOLLARS AND GET THE SHOW CANCELED.

WHY DON'T YOU JUST NOT WATCH THE SHOW?

THIS CLEAN, WHOLESOME TELEVISION! UGHH, IT MAKES ME SICK.

I NEVER LIKED ICE CREAM CONES TOO MUCH UNTIL I DISCOVERED A NEW WAY TO EAT THEM.

I BITE OFF THE BOTTOM OF THE CONE AND SUCK OUT THE ICE CREAM AS IT GETS SOFT.

YOU WOULDN'T BELIEVE SOME OF THE AWFUL NOISES YOU CAN MAKE, AND IT GETS PRETTY SLOPPY WHEN THE CONE GETS SOGGY AND BOTH ENDS START DRIPPING.

IN *MY* BOOK, FOOD SHOULD BE NUTRITION *AND* ENTERTAINMENT.

THAT'S WHY WE TIGERS LIKE OUR FOOD SURPRISED AND RUNNING.

I'M SO SMART IT'S ALMOST SCARY. I GUESS I'M A CHILD PROGENY.

MOST CHILDREN ARE.

HUH?

NOTHING.

PEOPLE THINK IT MUST BE FUN TO BE A SUPER GENIUS, BUT THEY DON'T REALIZE HOW HARD IT IS TO PUT UP WITH ALL THE IDIOTS IN THE WORLD.

ISN'T YOUR PANTS ZIPPER SUPPOSED TO BE IN THE FRONT?

WELL, THERE'S NO DELAYING THE INEVITABLE. LET'S GET IN THE CAR.

WHERE ARE WE GOING?

THE SAME PLACE WE GO *EVERY* SUMMER: CAMPING ON SOME DESOLATE ROCK AT THE END OF THE EARTH.

AGAIN?

YEP. THIS IS HOW DAD LIKES TO UNWIND.

WITH EVERYONE COMPLAINING?

RIGHT. HE LIKES TO WATCH US ALL SUFFER.

LOOK, DAD, THERE'S A TOWN COMING UP. SEE THE SIGN?

WHY DON'T WE PULL OFF, FIND A NICE MOTEL AND JUST STAY *THERE* FOR OUR VACATION? WE COULD SWIM IN THE POOL AND HAVE AIR CONDITIONING AND COLOR CABLE TV AND ROOM SERVICE!

NO ONE WOULD HAVE TO KNOW WE DIDN'T CAMP! *I* WOULDN'T TELL ANYONE! WE COULD EVEN GO TO THE STORE, BUY A BIG FISH, TAKE YOUR PICTURE WITH IT, AND SAY YOU CAUGHT IT! CAN'T WE, DAD? CAN'T WE TURN OFF HERE?

YES, LET'S!

NOW DON'T *YOU* START!

TA DA! WE'RE HERE!

GOOD OL' "ITCHY ISLAND," HOME OF THE NUCLEAR MOSQUITOES.

BUG BITES BUILD CHARACTER.

YEAH, AND LAST YEAR YOU SAID DIARRHEA BUILDS CHARACTER.

SO THINK WHAT A FINE YOUNG MAN YOU'RE GROWING UP TO BE.

...IF ALL THIS CHARACTER DOESN'T KILL ME FIRST.

THAT REMINDS ME, OPEN THE DUFFEL BAG AND GET OUT THE SPAM.

IF THE CANOE ISN'T HERE IN THE MORNING, IT MEANS HOBBES AND I STRUCK OUT FOR HOME.

Calvin and Hobbes

by WATTERSON

HEH HEH HEH...

YOU'RE IN TROUBLE *NOW*, HOBBES! HEH HEH HEH!

WHILE YOU HAVE JUST *ONE* WATER BALLOON, I HAVE *THREE*! I'M A WALKING ARSENAL OF HYDRO-WEAPONRY!

HA HA! I CAN SEE THE FEAR IN YOUR EYES! YOU REALIZE THAT I CAN GET YOU THREE TIMES WETTER THAN YOU CAN GET ME!

THROW YOUR BALLOON, AND YOUR UTTER SOGGINESS IS ASSURED! *I*, ON THE OTHER HAND, CAN ACT WITH IMPUNITY! WITH THREE BALLOONS, I FEAR NOTHING!

CATCH.

HEY! DON'T! MY ARMS ARE FULL!

OH NO!

SPLOOSH
GISSHH
SPLASH
FWOOSH

WE SUPER-POWERS HAVE IT TOUGH.

MAYBE YOU SHOULD STOCK UP ON BRAINS INSTEAD!

CALVIN and HOBBES
by WATTERSON

AHH... A DAY AT THE LAKE! THIS WILL BE GREAT!

I STILL DON'T SEE WHY WE CAN'T JUST SIT IN THE CAR WITH THE AIR CONDITIONER ON.

I'M GETTING SAND IN MY SUIT! I DON'T WANT TO SIT ON THE BEACH!

THIS WATER'S TOO COLD! I'M FREEZING TO DEATH!

OUT HERE THERE'S TOO MUCH SUN! I'LL GET SUNBURNED!

THIS LOTION MAKES ME GREASY AND MY SHIRT MAKES ME TOO HOT!

I DON'T WANT TO SIT IN THE SHADE! THIS IS BORING!

I HATE WALKING! MY LEGS ARE TIRED AND THE SAND IS TOO HOT AND THE WATER IS TOO COLD AND THERE'S NO SHADE HERE AND I'VE STILL GOT SAND IN MY SUIT!

WATTERSON

WHAT? ARE WE GOING ALREADY?

ARR! WE'RE BLOODTHIRSTY PIRATES!

AVAST, YE SCURVY DOGS! HOIST THE JOLLY ROGER AND READY THE PLANK!

HERE.

WHAT'S THIS?

OUR BOOTY!

HEY, MOM, DID YOU KNOW THAT GRAVITY IN OUTER SPACE WORKS AS IF SPACE WAS A SOFT, FLAT SURFACE? IT'S TRUE.

HEAVY MATTER, LIKE PLANETS, SINKS INTO THE SURFACE AND ANYTHING PASSING BY, LIKE LIGHT, WILL "ROLL" TOWARD THE DIP IN SPACE MADE BY THE PLANET. LIGHT IS ACTUALLY DEFLECTED BY GRAVITY! AMAZING, HUH?

AND SPEAKING OF GRAVITY, I DROPPED A PITCHER OF LEMONADE ON THE KITCHEN FLOOR WHEN MY ROLLER SKATES SLIPPED.

HOW CAN KIDS KNOW SO MUCH AND STILL BE SO DUMB?

YOU KNOW, THE WORLD SHOULD'VE BEEN DESIGNED SO EVERYONE DIDN'T HAVE TO EAT EACH OTHER TO SURVIVE. THERE SHOULD JUST BE FEWER PEOPLE AND ANIMALS TO BEGIN WITH.

AND THE WORLD CERTAINLY COULD'VE USED A MORE EVEN DISTRIBUTION OF ITS RESOURCES, THAT'S FOR SURE.

I WONDER WHY NOBODY CONSULTED YOU.

INCREDIBLE, ISN'T IT?

Panel 1: I PERFORMED A SCIENTIFIC EXPERIMENT TODAY.

Panel 2: YOU KNOW HOW MAPS ALWAYS SHOW NORTH AS UP AND SOUTH AS DOWN? I WANTED TO SEE IF THAT WAS TRUE OR NOT.

Panel 3: WHAT DID YOU FIND OUT? / NOT MUCH. YOUR COMPASS DIDN'T SURVIVE THE TRIP SOUTH FROM THE TOP OF THE TREE.

Panel 4: MY COMPASS?! / LET ME KNOW WHEN YOU GET A NEW ONE. MY JUNIOR SCIENTIST BOOK SAYS NOT TO GET DISCOURAGED BY TEMPORARY SETBACKS.

Panel 5: I'VE BEEN THINKING. YOU KNOW HOW BORING DAD IS? MAYBE IT'S A BIG PHONY ACT!

Panel 6: MAYBE AFTER HE PUTS US TO BED, DAD DONS SOME WEIRD COSTUME AND GOES OUT FIGHTING CRIME! MAYBE THIS WHOLE "DAD" STUFF IS JUST A SECRET IDENTITY!

Panel 7: MAYBE THE MAYOR CALLS DAD ON A SECRET HOT LINE WHENEVER THE CITY'S IN TROUBLE! MAYBE DAD'S A MASKED SUPERHERO!

Panel 8: IF THAT'S TRUE HE SHOULD DRIVE A COOLER CAR. / I KNOW. OURS DOESN'T EVEN HAVE A CASSETTE DECK.

Panel 9: THERE'S THE STEGOSAURUS OUT FRONT! THERE'S THE NATURAL HISTORY MUSEUM! HOORAY!

Panel 10: I CAN'T WAIT TO SEE ALL THE DINOSAURS! C'MON, LET'S HURRY!

Panel 11: IT'S CERTAINLY BEEN A WHILE SINCE WE'VE BEEN HERE, HASN'T IT?

Panel 12: AT THE MUSEUM'S REQUEST, YES. / OH, THAT'S RIGHT. CALVIN, NO BITING PEOPLE THIS TIME, REMEMBER? / RROWRR

WHAT KIND OF DINOSAUR DID YOU SAY THIS WAS?

IT'S A STEGO-SAURUS!

HE LOOKS PRETTY FEROCIOUS.

NO, HE WAS A PLANT EATER. THE TAIL SPIKES WERE FOR SELF-DEFENSE.

OH. DID TYRANNOSAURS FIGHT THESE?

OF COURSE NOT, MOM! TYRANNOSAURS CAME MILLIONS OF YEARS LATER!

LOOK, TRY NOT TO EMBARRASS ME WHEN WE GO INSIDE, OK?

WHY ARE WE GOING HERE IF HE ALREADY KNOWS EVERY-THING?

LOOK, HOBBES, HERE'S AN ANCESTOR OF *YOURS!* A SABER-TOOTHED TIGER!

HA HA, I'LL BET *HE* WAS POPULAR! IF ANYONE NEEDED TO OPEN A CAN OF JUICE, THEY'D JUST PUT HIM OVER IT AND HIT HIM ON THE HEAD! HA HA!

HEE HEE, I'LL BET THEY DIED OUT BECAUSE THEY COULDN'T UNDERSTAND EACH OTHER! THEY PWOBABBY DOKKED WIKE DIFF.' HA HA HA!

... ALL IN ALL, THOUGH, THEY WERE UNDOUBTEDLY THE PINNACLE OF PREHISTORIC EVOLUTION ..

LOOK, MOM, THE MUSEUM HAS A GIFT SHOP!

CAN I BUY SOMETHING? THEY'VE GOT DINOSAUR BOOKS, DINOSAUR MODELS, DINOSAUR T-SHIRTS, DINOSAUR POSTERS..

I DON'T THINK YOU NEED ANY MORE DINOSAUR STUFF, CALVIN.

BUT MOM, IT'S ALL *EDUCATIONAL!* YOU WANT ME TO *LEARN*, DON'T YOU??

BOY, SHE FELL FOR *THAT* ONE.

I'LL SAY! I WONDER IF WE COULD GET ANY BATMAN JUNK THIS WAY.

CALVIN AND HOBBES by WATTERSON

THERE! A FULL PITCHER OF "CALVIN'S CURATIVE ELIXIR"! WE'LL CHARGE PEOPLE A BUCK A GLASS AND GET RICH!

BUT THAT'S JUST DIRTY WATER FROM THE DRAINAGE DITCH! THERE ARE LEAVES IN IT!

"FORTIFIED WITH CHLOROPHYLL," WE'LL SAY.

NOBODY'S GOING TO PAY TO DRINK THAT! ANYONE CAN SEE IT'S FILTHY! IT'S SLUDGE!

HMM... MAYBE YOU'RE RIGHT.

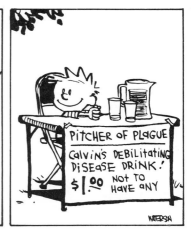

PITCHER OF PLAGUE
Calvin's DEBiLitating DISEASE DRINK!
$1.00 NOT TO HAVE ANY

I'VE DECIDED NOT TO GO TO SCHOOL THIS FALL.

I DON'T NEED AN EDUCATION. I DON'T NEED TO LEARN THINGS. I DON'T NEED TO DEVELOP SKILLS. IT'S TOO MUCH TROUBLE.

HOW ARE YOU GOING TO MAKE IT IN THE WORLD IF YOU DON'T KNOW ANYTHING AND YOU DON'T HAVE ANY SKILLS?!

I'LL GO ON TALK SHOWS AND HYPE MYSELF.

UGHH, THERE ARE TIMES WHEN I HATE OWNING A HOUSE. ALL THE MAINTENANCE!

THE WALLS NEED PAINTING, THE ROOF NEEDS TO BE FIXED, THE TREE OUT BACK NEEDS TO BE SPRAYED...

IT SEEMS LIKE THE WHOLE PLACE IS FALLING APART.

...AND WHAT ISN'T FALLING APART IS BEING ACTIVELY DESTROYED!

CALVIN AND HOBBES by WATTERSON

A 30-TON BRONTOSAURUS

... IS ABOUT TO FACE A PREMATURE EXTINCTION!

THE ALLOSAURUS, FEARSOME PREDATOR OF THE JURASSIC, STALKS HIS PREY!

THE HERD OF BRONTOSAURS IS UNAWARE OF HIS PRESENCE!

SPOTTING A STRAGGLER, THE ALLOSAURUS LUNGES!

THE BRONTOSAURUS REARS TO ITS FULL GIGANTIC HEIGHT!

WHAT INDUCES AN ALLOSAURUS TO ATTACK A MONSTER MORE THAN TWICE HIS OWN SIZE??

I'M HUNGRY!

THE HAMBURGERS ARE COOKING! NOW GET OFF ME!

CALVIN THE HUMMINGBIRD ZIPS BY WITH A LOUD WHIR!

ALTHOUGH SMALL, HE PUTS OUT TREMENDOUS ENERGY. TO HOVER, HIS WINGS BEAT HUNDREDS OF TIMES EACH SECOND!

WHAT FUELS THIS INCREDIBLE METABOLISM? CONCENTRATED SUGAR WATER! HE DRINKS HALF HIS WEIGHT A DAY!

...PREFERABLY LOADED WITH CAFFEINE.

ARE YOU DRINKING MORE SODA POP?!

SLURRPP

"ONCE UPON A TIME THERE WAS..."

HOLD IT.

WHAT'S THE MATTER?

HAS THIS BOOK BEEN A BEST SELLER? HAS THE AUTHOR WON A PULITZER? DID THE NEW YORK TIMES LIKE IT?

I ONLY WANT STORIES THAT COME HIGHLY RECOMMENDED. ARE THERE ANY LAUDATORY QUOTES ON THE DUST JACKET?

AHEM... "ONCE UPON A TIME THERE WAS A NOISY KID WHO STARTED GOING TO BED WITHOUT A STORY."

HAS THIS BOOK BEEN MADE INTO A MOVIE? COULD WE BE WATCHING THIS ON VIDEO?

WHAT ARE YOU DOING?

I'M PRACTICING MY SNEERS.

THERE'S NOTHING LIKE A GOOD SNEER TO DRY UP CONVERSATION. HOW'S MINE LOOK?

AWFUL!

THANKS. WITH THIS SNEER, I HOPE TO BE AN UNBEARABLE BURDEN AT ANY SOCIAL OCCASION.

THAT WILL GIVE YOU A REAL HEAD START ON BEING A TEEN-AGER.

I KNOW! IT'S LIKE GETTING SEVEN EXTRA YEARS!

MOM WANTS ME TO MAKE MY BED. COME HELP ME, OK?

OK.

YOU GET SOME PENCILS, AND I'LL GET SOME BIG PAPER!

I THOUGHT WE WERE MAKING THE BED.

AND DO ALL THAT WORK?!? NO, WE'RE GOING TO INVENT A ROBOT TO MAKE THE BED *FOR* US!

WON'T INVENTING A ROBOT BE MORE WORK THAN MAKING THE BED?

IT'S ONLY WORK IF SOMEBODY MAKES YOU DO IT.

HOW ARE WE GOING TO INVENT A ROBOT? WE DON'T KNOW ANYTHING ABOUT MACHINES.

MAYBE *YOU* DON'T.

IT'S EASY. THERE ARE JUST FOUR SIMPLE MACHINES TO ALTER FORCE: THE LEVER, THE PULLEY, THE INCLINED PLANE AND, UM, THE INTERNAL COMBUSTION ENGINE.

TAKE MY WORD FOR IT, I'M AN EXPERT AT INVENTIONS.

SO WHERE DO WE START?

WE ASK MOM FOR A RESEARCH GRANT.

HI, MOM. CAN I LOOK AT YOUR WALLET FOR A FEW MINUTES? I, UH, WANT TO SEE SOMETHING.

HOLD ON. DID YOU MAKE YOUR BED LIKE I ASKED YOU?

I'M WORKING ON IT.

AS I RECALL, YOUR BED IS IN YOUR ROOM.

I'M INVENTING A ROBOT TO MAKE THE BED, BUT I NEED A GRANT. CAN I HAVE $50?

WHAT'D SHE SAY? DID YOU GET THE MONEY?

BOY, WHEN WE'RE THE COVER STORY OF POPULAR MECHANICS, I'LL HAVE SOME CHOICE WORDS TO SAY ABOUT FAMILY ENCOURAGEMENT.

OK, THE FIRST THING OUR ROBOT NEEDS IS A HEAD.

SHOULD WE USE A COFFEE CAN?

NO, THAT'S TOO SMALL. THE HEAD HAS TO HOLD THIS TAPE RECORDER. SEE, I'VE MADE RECORDINGS FOR THE ROBOT'S VOICE!

REALLY?

SURE! THIS WAY, OUR ROBOT NOT ONLY COMMUNICATES, BUT WE CAN ALSO "PROGRAM" HIM TO HAVE THE PROPER PERSONALITY!

PERSONALITY?

RIGHT. ROBOTS SHOULD BE *RESPECTFUL*.

CLICK HOW MAY I EASE YOUR LIFE, OH GRAND EXALTED MASTER?

HEY, DAD, I'M INVENTING A ROBOT. CAN YOU GET ME A PATENT?

YOU INVENTED A ROBOT?

WELL, HERE IT IS SO FAR. HOBBES AND I HAVE BEEN WORKING ON IT ALL AFTERNOON. IT'S NOT QUITE PERFECTED YET, BUT YOU GET THE IDEA.

HMM...WHAT DOES IT DO?

THAT'S THE PROBLEM. WE HAVEN'T FIGURED OUT HOW TO MAKE IT DO WHAT WE WANT.

DON'T GET DISCOURAGED. YOUR MOM AND I GOT THE SAME RESULTS AFTER WORKING ON *YOU* FOR SIX *YEARS*.

HAR HAR. MY ATTORNEY IS A COMEDIAN.

WELL, HOBBES, WE MIGHT AS WELL GIVE UP. I CAN'T FIGURE OUT HOW TO MAKE A ROBOT. THIS ONE DOESN'T DO ANYTHING.

IT'S PAST YOUR BEDTIME, CALVIN. YOU'LL HAVE TO LEAVE YOUR TOYS FOR TOMORROW.

OK, MOM. OUR ROBOT WASN'T WORKING OUT ANY-WAY.

GOSH, AND WE SPENT ALL DAY ON IT, TOO. I THOUGHT FOR SURE OUR ROBOT WOULD SAVE US FROM MAKING THE BED.

AND IN A WAY, HE *DID!*

HEY, YEAH! WE'RE GENIUSES!

YOUR MOM SURE WAS CHEERFUL THIS MORNING.

HMPH.

I'VE NEVER SEEN HER HUMMING AND SASHAYING AROUND THE KITCHEN LIKE THAT.

HMPH.

HOW LONG HAVE WE BEEN WAITING FOR THE BUS NOW?

ABOUT TWO AND A HALF HOURS.

I THINK MOM PUT ME OUT HERE THIS EARLY ON *PURPOSE.*

HI, CALVIN! AREN'T YOU EXCITED ABOUT GOING TO SCHOOL? LOOK AT ALL THESE GREAT SCHOOL SUPPLIES I GOT! I LOVE HAVING NEW NOTEBOOKS AND STUFF!

ALL *I'VE* GOT TO SAY IS THEY'RE NOT MAKING *ME* LEARN ANY FOREIGN LANGUAGES! IF ENGLISH IS GOOD ENOUGH FOR *ME,* THEN BY GOLLY, IT'S GOOD ENOUGH FOR THE *REST* OF THE WORLD!

EVERYONE SHOULD SPEAK ENGLISH OR JUST SHUT UP, THAT'S WHAT *I* SAY!

YOU SHOULD MAYBE CHECK THE CHEMICAL CONTENT OF YOUR BREAKFAST CEREAL.

THEY CAN MAKE ME GO UNTIL GRADE EIGHT, AND THEN, *FFFT,* I'M OUTTA HERE!

CALVIN, WOULD YOU LEAD THE CLASS IN THE PLEDGE OF ALLEGIANCE?

NO!

WHAT DID THE SUPREME COURT DECIDE ABOUT THAT? IS THIS A PRAYER? DON'T YOU HAVE TO READ ME MY RIGHTS? I DON'T KEEP UP WITH THIS STUFF! I'M JUST A KID!

I'M ONLY HERE BECAUSE MY PARENTS MAKE ME GO! I DON'T WANT TO BE A TEST CASE! I DON'T EVEN KNOW WHAT COURT DISTRICT I'M IN! CALL ON SOMEONE ELSE!

CALVIN?

SIGHHHH I CAN'T BELIEVE IT'S NOT EVEN 8:15 YET.

THE FEARLESS SPACEMAN SPIFF IS BEING PURSUED ACROSS THE GALAXY BY DREADED SCUM BEINGS!

THEY'RE GAINING! SPIFF'S ONLY CHANCE TO LOSE THEM IS TO RELEASE A GIANT SMOKE CLOUD BEHIND HIS SPACECRAFT! OUR HERO THROWS THE LEVER!

HEH HEH... JUST UH, CLAPPING THE ERASERS, HEH HEH... (COUGH)

YOU AGAIN?

* SIGHHHH *
I CAN'T BELIEVE IT'S NOT EVEN 8:30 YET.

WHAT A DAY.

I'M HO-O-AAAH!

KAPOINWW!!!

THINGS GET SO DARN QUIET WHEN YOU'RE NOT AROUND.

THERE'S GOING TO BE SOME RUCKUS *NOW*, BUDDY-BOY!

IS IT? IT *IS*! IT'S **SATURDAY**! OH BOY!

NO SCHOOL! NO HOMEWORK! JUST CARTOONS AND FUN THE WHOLE DAY LONG!

HOORAY!

TURN ON THE TV! GET OUT THE CEREAL! IT'S SAAAAT URDAY!

BONK
BONK
BONK

YOU'RE GETTING UP?? IT'S BARELY LIGHT OUT!

I'M GOING TO THE OFFICE AND GET SOME SLEEP.

Calvin and Hobbes
by WATTERSON

CALVIN?
CALVIN?
CALVIN!

HMM... THE ENGINE'S MAKING FUNNY NOISES..

SPACEMAN SPIFF IS GOING DOWN OVER PLANET GORK!

ZOUNDS! THE PLANET IS INHABITED! AN ALIEN METROPOLIS OPENS UP BEFORE OUR HERO'S EYES!

SPIFF'S STABILIZERS REFUSE TO RESPOND! OUR HERO IS GOING TO CRASH!

THIS SPELLS DISASTER!

CALVIN!

"UH... D...I...S...A... S...T...E...R.

VERY GOOD. I'M GLAD YOU WERE PAYING ATTENTION.

YES! ONCE AGAIN THE INCREDIBLE SPACEMAN SPIFF BEATS ALL ODDS TO SAVE THE DAY!

YOU MAY SIT DOWN, CALVIN.

UH OH, CALVIN THE REPTILE IS IN TROUBLE!

AS AN ECTOTHERM, HIS BODY RELIES ON THE ENVIRONMENT TO WARM OR COOL ITS TEMPERATURE.

NOW THAT IT'S COLDER OUTSIDE, CALVIN'S BODY TEMPERATURE FALLS AND HE BECOMES SLUGGISH! HE'LL GO INTO TORPOR IF HE CAN'T FIND A WARM PLACE TO LIE!

LEAVE THE THERMOSTAT ALONE, AND PUT ON A SWEATER IF YOU'RE COLD.

I...I DON'T HAVE THE EN..ENERGY!

I HEARD THAT BIG CATS DON'T PURR.

THAT'S TRUE. WE'RE TOO FIERCE AND FEROCIOUS. WE DON'T EVER PURR.

WELL WHAT DO YOU CALL THE NOISE YOU MAKE WHEN YOU GET YOUR TUMMY RUBBED?!

GROWLING FRIENDLY-LIKE.

CALVIN, YOUR MOM AND I LOOKED OVER YOUR REPORT CARD, AND WE THINK YOU COULD BE DOING BETTER.

BUT I DON'T LIKE SCHOOL.

WHY NOT? YOU LIKE TO READ AND YOU LIKE TO LEARN. I KNOW YOU DO.

I MEAN, YOU'VE READ EVERY DINOSAUR BOOK EVER WRITTEN, AND YOU'VE LEARNED A LOT, RIGHT? READING AND LEARNING ARE FUN.

YEAH..

SO WHY DON'T YOU LIKE SCHOOL?

WE DON'T READ ABOUT DINOSAURS.

CALVIN AND HOBBES

by WATTERSON

PHWPPT!

THPWIPBTH

AHHH..

DEAR, SOMETIME I WANT YOU TO LOOK AT THAT DISCOLORED SPOT ON THE RUG. IT SEEMS TO BE GETTING BIGGER ALL THE TIME.

MAY I LEAVE THE TABLE? LIKE RIGHT NOW?

I want that truck, Twinky.

IT'S MINE, MOE. I BROUGHT IT FROM HOME.

I said gimme the truck.

MOE, YOU CAN'T JUST *TAKE* THINGS FROM PEOPLE BECAUSE YOU'RE BIGGER!

I'm not taking it. You're **giving** it to me because we'll both be so much happier that way.

HOW TOUCHING.

MOE, GIVE ME MY TRUCK BACK. IT'S NOT YOURS.

It is **now**. You gave it to me.

I DIDN'T HAVE MUCH CHOICE, *DID* I?! IT WAS EITHER GIVE UP THE TRUCK OR GET PUNCHED!

So?

SO I ONLY "GAVE" IT TO YOU BECAUSE YOU'RE BIGGER AND MEANER THAN ME!

Yeah? ...So?

THE FORENSIC MARVEL HAS REDUCED MY LOGIC TO SHAMBLES.

You're saying you changed your mind about getting punched?

THAT NO-GOOD, ROTTEN MOE! HE WON'T GIVE MY TRUCK BACK TO ME. THE OAF WILL PROBABLY BREAK IT, TOO.

SHOULD I STEAL IT BACK? I KNOW STEALING IS WRONG, BUT *HE* STOLE IT FROM *ME*, AND IF I **DON'T** STEAL IT BACK, MOE WILL JUST KEEP IT, AND THAT'S NOT FAIR.

THEY SAY TWO WRONGS DON'T MAKE A RIGHT, BUT WHAT ARE YOU SUPPOSED TO *DO* THEN? JUST LET THE BIGGEST GUY MAKE HIS OWN RULES ALL THE TIME? LET MIGHT MAKE RIGHT?

... THAT SOUNDS REASONABLE.

BY GOLLY, I *AM* GOING TO STEAL MY TRUCK BACK FROM MOE! IT'S MINE AND HE HAS NO RIGHT TO HAVE IT!

I'LL JUST SNEAK UP BEHIND THE SWINGS HERE, AND WHEN MOE'S NOT LOOKING, I'LL RUN UP, GRAB THE TRUCK AND TAKE OFF!

THIS PLAYGROUND SHOULD HAVE ONE OF THOSE AUTOMATIC INSURANCE MACHINES LIKE THEY HAVE IN AIRPORTS.

OK, MOE'S GOT HIS BACK TO ME! NOW I'LL ZIP OVER, STEAL MY TRUCK BACK AND RUN LIKE CRAZY!

HE'LL NEVER KNOW WHAT HIT HIM! BY THE TIME HE SEES THE TRUCK IS GONE, I'LL BE A MILE AWAY! IT'S A FAIL-PROOF PLAN! NOTHING CAN GO WRONG! IT'S A SNAP!

THERE'S NO REASON TO HESITATE. IT'LL BE OVER IN A SPLIT SECOND, AND I'LL SURE BE GLAD TO HAVE MY TRUCK BACK! I'LL JUST DO IT AND BE DONE! NOTHING TO IT! IT'S EASY!

OBVIOUSLY MY BODY DOESN'T BELIEVE A WORD MY BRAIN IS SAYING.

PHOOEY, WHO AM I KIDDING? I'D NEVER GET AWAY WITH STEALING MY TRUCK BACK FROM MOE. THE UGLY GALOOT IS THE SIZE OF A BUICK.

HMM... SINCE I CAN'T *FIGHT* HIM, MAYBE I SHOULD TRY *TALKING* TO HIM. MAYBE IF I REASONED WITH HIM, HE'D SEE *MY* SIDE.

MAYBE HE'D REALIZE THAT STEALING HURTS PEOPLE, AND MAYBE HE'D RETURN MY TRUCK *WILLINGLY.*

MAYBE IF I'M REALLY LUCKY I WON'T GO THROUGH LIFE WITH THE NICKNAME "OMELET FACE."

HAVE YOU SEEN MY SHOES? I THOUGHT I HAD THEM OUT RIGHT HERE.

YOUR SHOES? I DON'T KNOW.

THEY *WERE* RIGHT HERE. WHERE COULD THEY HAVE GONE?

WE'RE GOING TO BE LATE.

WELL I CAN'T GO ANYWHERE WITHOUT MY *SHOES*. HELP ME LOOK.

THEY'RE NOT LEAVING *US* WITH A BABY SITTER TONIGHT!

DING DONG

IT'S *ROSALYN!*

ANSWER THE DOOR, WILL YOU PLEASE, CALVIN?

HI ROZ. MY PARENTS CHANGED THEIR MINDS ABOUT GOING OUT, SO WE WON'T BE NEEDING YOUR SERVICES. GOODBYE.

HI, ROSALYN. WHAT ARE YOU TALKING ABOUT, CALVIN?

YOU CAN'T GO OUT IF MOM CAN'T FIND HER *SHOES*, RIGHT?

AND WHAT DO *YOU* KNOW ABOUT *THAT?*

UH, NOTHING! HA HA! UM, WHY? ARE HER SHOES MISSING?

I'D LIKE TO BE PAID IN ADVANCE TONIGHT.

PHOOEY. MOM AND DAD LEFT. NOW WE'RE HERE ALONE WITH THE BABY SITTER FROM THE BLACK LAGOON.

HEE HEE! DO YOU THINK SHE REMEMBERS HOW LAST TIME WE THREATENED TO FLUSH HER SCIENCE NOTES DOWN THE TOILET?

HA HA HA! OUR FINEST MOMENT!

OK, YOU, GET IN BED.

WHAT?! IT'S NOT EVEN 6:30!

SHE REMEMBERS, ALL RIGHT.

SHE CAN'T GET AWAY WITH THIS. WE'LL CALL THE RESCUE SQUAD.

WOW, THIS IS FUN! ALL THE TV SHOWS WE'RE NOT ALLOWED TO WATCH, AND A BAG OF COOKIES EACH!

BLAM! BLAM! SCREEEEECHH!

SLAM!

HEY, WHAT WAS THAT?

AAUGH!! ROSALYN! H-HOW DID YOU G-GET IN??

GULP WHOOPS, I THINK IT'S PAST MY BEDTIME.

IT WAS ALL A MISUNDERSTANDING! AN INNOCENT MISTAKE! LET ME EXPLAIN!

CALVIN, LISTEN CLOSELY. LOCKING ROSALYN OUT OF THE HOUSE WASN'T JUST *MEAN*, IT WAS *DANGEROUS*. IF YOU'D HURT YOURSELF OR IF THERE WAS A FIRE, SHE WOULDN'T HAVE BEEN ABLE TO HELP YOU.

YOU GO APOLOGIZE TO ROSALYN RIGHT NOW.

I-I'M SORRY, ROSALYN.

AND WE'RE SORRY TOO. I *PROMISE* YOU CALVIN WILL BEHAVE HIMSELF NEXT TIME.

AN EXTRA FIVE WOULD HELP THERE *BE* A NEXT TIME.

BOY, DID I GET IN TROUBLE.

STEALING MOM'S SHOES AND MAKING MOM AND DAD LATE... THEN LOCKING THE BABY SITTER OUT OF THE HOUSE... WHOOF.

THAT'S A LOT TO LIVE DOWN FOR JUST ONE EVENING. I FEEL PRETTY BAD.

AND HAVING EATEN A WHOLE PACKAGE OF OREOS DOESN'T HELP.

YOU SAID IT.

GISZH! ... GISZH! ...

..GISZH!

OH, NO! IT'S THE MIDDLE OF RECESS AND THERE'S A TYRANNOSAURUS ON THE PLAYGROUND!

THE KIDS AT THE TOP OF THE SLIDE ARE THE FIRST TO GO! HOW IRONIC THAT THEY HAD PUSHED AND FOUGHT EACH OTHER TO BE THERE!

PANDEMONIUM ENSUES! TEACHERS LINE THE KIDS UP TO GO INSIDE, BUT THAT PROVES TO BE A SAD MISTAKE!

WALKING QUIETLY IN SINGLE FILE, THE KIDS ARE GOBBLED UP LIKE CHILDREN McNUGGETS!

SOON THE PLAYGROUND IS EMPTY! IT'S ALL HIS! THE TYRANNOSAUR LETS OUT A TRIUMPHANT ROAR!

SAY, WHERE'S CALVIN? RECESS IS OVER. DIDN'T HE SEE US LINE UP TO COME IN?

I SEE HIM, MISS WORMWOOD! HE'S OUT BY THE SWINGS AND HE'S YELLING OR SOMETHING!

STUPENDOUS MAN CIRCLES THE EARTH WITH A 200-INCH TELESCOPE LENS!

ALIGNED PERFECTLY WITH THE SUN, THE MAGNIFYING LENS FOCUSES THE TERRIBLE SOLAR ENERGY...

...AND FRIES A CERTAIN ELEMENTARY SCHOOL CLEAN OFF THE MAP!

NOW MILD-MANNERED CALVIN HAS NO NEED TO DO HIS HOMEWORK EVER AGAIN! LIBERTY PREVAILS!

HOW'S YOUR HOMEWORK COMING, CALVIN?

UH OH, IT'S MY ARCH-NEMESIS, MOM-LADY! SHE CAN'T DISCOVER MY SECRET IDENTITY!

CALVIN? ARE YOU DOING YOUR HOMEWORK IN THERE?

QUICKLY, STUPENDOUS MAN LEAPS INTO THE CLOSET TO CHANGE BACK INTO HIS 6-YEAR-OLD ALTER EGO, MILD-MANNERED CALVIN!

CALVIN? ARE YOU IN HERE?

UNFORTUNATELY, STUPENDOUS MAN'S CAPE IS CAUGHT IN MILD-MANNERED CALVIN'S ZIPPER! CURSES!

THIS IS GOING TO BE A GOOD ONE, I CAN TELL.

GEEZ, MOM! CAN'T A GUY HAVE A LITTLE PRIVACY?!

AND WHY, MAY I ASK, ARE YOU STANDING IN YOUR UNDERWEAR IN THE CLOSET?

OH, NO REASON. UM... I WAS HOT.

YOU'RE SUPPOSED TO BE DOING YOUR HOMEWORK!

I DON'T NEED TO DO IT NOW, THANKS TO STUPENDOUS MAN!

OH YEAH?

IT WAS GREAT! HE FRIED THE SCHOOL WITH A BIG MAGNIFYING LENS IN SPACE! I'M SURE IT WILL BE IN ALL THE PAPERS TOMORROW.

BOY, SHE'LL BE IN TROUBLE WHEN SHE GIVES ME MY COSTUME BACK. BIG TROUBLE.

CALVIN AND HOBBES by WATTERSON

I'M HO-OME!

HI, CALVIN. WHATCHA DOIN'?

OOF, GET THIS BIG LUMMOX OFF ME.

LOOK AT YOU! YOU DIDN'T EVEN CHANGE OUT OF YOUR SCHOOL CLOTHES!

HOW COULD I?! I DIDN'T EVEN GET IN THE DOOR!

EVERY DAY THIS MANIAC IS SO GLAD TO SEE ME THAT HE BLASTS OUT LIKE A BIG ORANGE TORPEDO! A *DOG* WILL JUST WAG ITS TAIL, BUT OF COURSE A *TIGER* HAS TO *POUNCE* ON YOU! STUPID ANIMAL!

HE POUNCES ON YOU?

OH, AND DON'T THINK HE DOESN'T ENJOY THE CUNNING AND TREACHERY OF IT ALL! TIGERS *LIVE* FOR THE THRILL OF A SNEAK ATTACK! IT'S THEIR EVIL NATURE!

HE'S JUST SITTING THERE.

OH, SURE, *BIG* DISGUISE! LIKE NO ONE CAN FATHOM THE SAVAGE MIND OF A JUNGLE CAT! HA! HE'S A KILLER TO THE CORE!

I WISH MY PARENTS WOULD MOVE. MY DIARY IS GETTING WEIRDER EVERY DAY.

YEAH, *YOU* KNOW WHO I'M TALKING ABOUT! WIPE OFF THAT GRIN OR I'LL DO IT *FOR* YOU!

I'VE GOT AN IDEA, DAD.

MAYBE I'D GET BETTER GRADES IF YOU OFFERED ME $1 FOR EVERY "D", $5 FOR EVERY "C", $10 FOR EVERY "B", AND $50 FOR EVERY "A"!

I'M NOT GOING TO *BRIBE* YOU, CALVIN. YOU SHOULD APPLY YOURSELF FOR YOUR OWN GOOD.

RATS. I THOUGHT I COULD MAKE AN EASY FOUR BUCKS.

HELLO? VALLEY HARDWARE? YES, I'M CALLING TO SEE IF YOU SELL BLASTING CAPS, DETONATORS, TIMERS AND WIRE.

JUST THE WIRE? OK, FORGET IT. DO YOU RENT BULLDOZERS OR BACKHOES?

NO, NO, A ROTOTILLER WON'T DO AT ALL. I NEED SOMETHING MORE LIKE A WRECKING BALL. DO YOU KNOW WHERE I COULD GET ANYTHING LIKE THAT? NO? OK, GOODBYE.

LOOKS LIKE ANOTHER BORING DAY, HOBBES.

I CAN'T SLEEP, HOBBES. I'VE BEEN THINKING.

WHAT ABOUT?

WELL, SUPPOSE THERE'S NO AFTERLIFE. THAT WOULD MEAN *THIS* LIFE IS ALL YOU GET.

AND *THAT* WOULD MEAN I'M SITTING HERE IN BED AS PRECIOUS MOMENTS OF MY ALL-TOO-SHORT LIFE DISAPPEAR FOREVER.

HONEY, WAKE UP. DO YOU HEAR THE TELEVISION ON?

Calvin and Hobbes

by WATTERSON

GOSH, IT'S 1:30 AND I'M STILL AWAKE.

SOMEONE MUST'VE WAYLAID MR. SANDMAN.

I JUST CAN'T... GET... COMFORTABLE.

MMF.

I'M EXHAUSTED, BUT I CAN'T FALL ASLEEP.

MAYBE IF I JUST LIE STILL AND THINK ABOUT HOW GOOD IT FEELS TO BE IN BED, AND HOW SOFT THE PILLOW IS, AND HOW VERY, VERY TIRED I AM...

...PHOOEY, THIS ISN'T WORKING. ALL I WANT IS TO GET SOME SLEEP. THIS IS AWFUL.

CALVIN?

GEE MOM, ARE YOU AWAKE TOO?

IT'S TIME TO GET UP.

IT **CAN'T** BE! IT'S THE MIDDLE OF THE NIGHT AND I HAVEN'T SLEPT A WINK YET!

CALVIN?

C'MON, UP AND AT 'EM.

HUZBGH

blink
blink

THIS IS GOING TO BE A BAD DAY.

THE STRANGEST THING HAPPENED TO ME A FEW MINUTES AGO.

OH? WHAT?

I WAS MINDING MY OWN BUSINESS, WHEN SUDDENLY I WAS ZAPPED INTO SOME SORT OF SPACE VOID VORTEX!

THERE I WATCHED HELPLESSLY AS AN EVIL DUPLICATE OF MYSELF FROM A PARALLEL UNIVERSE TOOK MY PLACE ON EARTH, AND...

WHAT HAVE YOU DONE *NOW*?

NO, NO, SEE, IT WASN'T *ME*...

HEH HEH HEH!

AHA! I SEE YOU! SNEAKING UP TO POUNCE ON ME, EH?

PHOOEY.

YOU SEE WHY *MOST* TIGERS DON'T CHUCKLE TO THEMSELVES.

WANT TO PLAY A GREAT GAME I INVENTED?

OK.

IT'S CALLED "GROSS OUT." YOU SAY THE GROSSEST THING YOU CAN IMAGINE, AND THEN I TRY TO THINK OF SOMETHING EVEN GROSSER.

WHOEVER COMES UP WITH THE GROSSEST THING GETS A POINT, AND WE PLAY UNTIL SOMEONE GETS 50 POINTS, OK?

I THINK I ALREADY KNOW WHO'S GOING TO WIN.

IT'S WEIRD. NOBODY HAS EVER PLAYED A WHOLE GAME WITH ME.

WHAT AM I GOING TO DO ABOUT THIS REPORT ON BATS? YOU'VE GOT TO HELP ME, HOBBES!

OK, ...UM, FIRST LET'S MAKE A LIST OF WHAT WE KNOW.

YEAH! THAT'S A GOOD WAY TO START! GREAT!

NUMBER ONE: WHAT ARE BATS?

THEY'RE BUGS, AREN'T THEY? YEAH, PUT THAT DOWN.

#1 Bats = Bugs

ARE YOU SURE?

THEY FLY, RIGHT? THEY'RE UGLY AND HAIRY, RIGHT? C'MON, THIS IS TAKING ALL DAY!

WATTERSON

I THINK WE'VE GOT ENOUGH INFORMATION NOW, DON'T YOU?

ALL WE HAVE IS ONE "FACT" YOU MADE UP.

THAT'S PLENTY. BY THE TIME WE ADD AN INTRODUCTION, A FEW ILLUSTRATIONS, AND A CONCLUSION, IT WILL LOOK LIKE A GRADUATE THESIS.

BESIDES, I'VE GOT A SECRET WEAPON THAT WILL *GUARANTEE* ME A GOOD GRADE! NO TEACHER CAN RESIST *THIS*!

WHAT IS IT?

A CLEAR PLASTIC BINDER! PRETTY PROFESSIONAL LOOKING, EH?

I DON'T WANT CO-AUTHOR CREDIT ON THIS, OK?

WATTERSON

HI SUSIE! DID YOU WRITE YOUR REPORT?

YEAH, I SPENT ALL LAST EVENING ON IT. DID YOU?

WATTERSON

WELL, WHEN YOU KNOW AS MUCH AS *I* DO, IT DOESN'T TAKE AS LONG. MINE TOOK ABOUT 15 MINUTES.

15 MINUTES?! LET'S SEE.

I GUESS YOU WON'T BE SETTING THE GRADE CURVE *THIS* TIME, SUSIE! READ IT AND WEEP.

"BATS: THE BIG BUG SCOURGE OF THE SKIES."

NOTE THE PROFESSIONAL CLEAR PLASTIC BINDER.

BATS AREN'T *BUGS*!

ALL RIGHT, CLASS, WHO WOULD LIKE TO GIVE HIS REPORT FIRST?

I WOULD! I WOULD!

WHY CALVIN, WHAT A SURPRISE TO SEE *YOU* VOLUNTEER! YOU MUST HAVE DONE A GOOD JOB. GO TO THE FRONT OF THE CLASS.

OH BOY!

NOW LET'S ALL PAY ATTENTION. GO AHEAD, CALVIN.

THANK YOU. BEFORE I BEGIN, I'D LIKE EVERYONE TO NOTICE THAT MY REPORT IS IN A PROFESSIONAL, CLEAR PLASTIC BINDER.

THAT'S VERY NICE. GO AHEAD.

WHEN A REPORT LOOKS THIS GOOD, YOU KNOW IT'LL GET AN "A". THAT'S A TIP, KIDS, WRITE IT DOWN.

MY REPORT IS ON BATS. ...AHEM...

"DUSK! WITH A CREEPY, TINGLING SENSATION, YOU HEAR THE FLUTTERING OF LEATHERY WINGS! *BATS!* WITH GLOWING RED EYES AND GLISTENING FANGS, THESE UNSPEAKABLE GIANT BUGS DROP ONTO..."

BATS AREN'T BUGS!!

LOOK, WHO'S GIVING THE REPORT? *YOU* CHONDERHEADS ...OR *ME*?!

CALVIN, I'D LIKE TO SEE YOU A MOMENT.

MAN ALIVE! CAN YOU BELIEVE WHAT MY TEACHER WROTE ON MY REPORT?

SHE SAYS I OBVIOUSLY DID NO RESEARCH WHATSOEVER ON BATS AND THAT MY SCIENTIFIC ILLUSTRATION LOOKS LIKE I TRACED THE BATMAN LOGO AND ADDED FANGS!

SHE'S PRETTY PERCEPTIVE.

SHE DIDN'T EVEN GIVE ME CREDIT FOR MY PROFESSIONAL CLEAR PLASTIC BINDER!

WHAT DID YOUR PARENTS HAVE TO SAY?

NOTHING. AND IF YOU'LL GIVE ME A HAND HERE, IT WILL STAY THAT WAY.

Calvin and Hobbes

by WATTERSON

I SURE WISH IT WOULD SNOW.

WHAT'S WITH THE SLED? THERE'S NO SNOW.

I AIM TO FIX *THAT* RIGHT NOW WITH AN APPEAL TO THE SNOW DEMONS.

SNOW DEMONS?

OBVIOUSLY THEY'RE TORMENTING US WITH THIS WIMPY WEATHER BECAUSE THEY'RE ANGRY. WE MUST APPEASE THEM.

OH.

I'M GOING TO LIE HERE ON MY SLED AND THINK SNOW THOUGHTS UNTIL THE SNOW DEMONS HAVE MERCY AND UNLEASH A BLIZZARD.

SNOW, SNOW! HIGH AND LOW! WHEREVER WE GO! LET IT BLOW! TO AND FRO! HI-DE-HO! SNOW! SNOW! SNOW!

WELL, I'LL COME OUT IN EARLY JANUARY AND SEE HOW YOU'RE DOING.

TELL MOM I'LL NEED MY MEALS OUT HERE AND I WON'T BE GOING TO SCHOOL TOMORROW.

Calvin and Hobbes

by WATTERSON

SIGHHHH...

HEY! WHOA! WHOAA!

WAHH!

BAM

CALVIN, QUIT BANGING AROUND!

OW! WHAT AM I DOING ON THE CEILING?

HMM... NOTHING ELSE FELL UP. JUST ME. THIS IS VERY STRANGE.

EVEN IF I TRY TO JUMP TO THE FLOOR, I LAND BACK ON THE CEILING! MY PERSONAL GRAVITY MUST HAVE REVERSED POLARITY!

YOU'D THINK THIS WOULD BE THE TYPE OF THING WE'D LEARN ABOUT IN SCIENCE CLASS, BUT NO, WE LEARN ABOUT CIRRUS CLOUDS.

HAVING MY PERSONAL GRAVITY POLARITY REVERSED IS A REAL NUISANCE. HOW AM I GOING TO GET UP TO THE FLOOR?

THERE'S NOT ANYTHING ON THE CEILING THAT I COULD EVEN CLIMB UP.

HOW AM I SUPPOSED TO DO MY HOMEWORK WHEN I'M TRAPPED ON THE CEILING? IT'S IMPOSSIBLE.

MOM AND DAD WON'T BE TOO HAPPY ABOUT *THIS*. NO SIR.

DAD WILL HAVE TO BOLT MY BED TO THE CEILING TONIGHT, AND MOM WILL HAVE TO STAND ON A STEPLADDER TO HAND ME DINNER.

THEN I'LL HAVE TO HOLD MY PLATE UPSIDE-DOWN ABOVE MY HEAD AND SCRAPE THE FOOD OFF THE UNDERSIDE! AND IF I SPILL ANYTHING, IT WILL FLY 10 FEET UP TO THE FLOOR AND SPLOT!

THIS IS GOING TO BE THE MOST FUN I'VE EVER HAD!

ALL THIS WIDE OPEN CEILING SPACE! I WISH I COULD GET MY ROLLER SKATES.

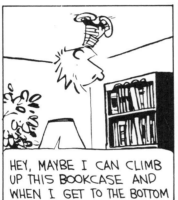

HEY, MAYBE I CAN CLIMB UP THIS BOOKCASE AND WHEN I GET TO THE BOTTOM SHELF, LEAP TO A CHAIR!

THEN I CAN PULL MYSELF ACROSS TO OTHER PIECES OF FURNITURE AND WORK MY WAY TO MY TOY CHEST.

...I CAN HEAR MOM NOW: "HOW ON EARTH DID YOU GET SNEAKER PRINTS ON THE UNDERSIDE OF EACH SHELF?!"

THERE! I THINK I CAN JUMP TO THAT CHAIR AND HANG ONTO THE BACK.

GEERONIMOOO!

¡WHOAAA!

WHAM!

GREAT. JUST GREAT.

CALVIN, QUIT BANGING AROUND!

RRG! MMF!

GETTING ANY **HOMEWORK** DONE, OR ARE YOU JUST RUINING FURNITURE?

MAYBE I'M HANGING HERE FOR DEAR **LIFE!** EVER THINK OF **THAT?**

I'M **TELLING** YOU, MY PERSONAL GRAVITY REVERSED ITS POLARITY! I FALL **UP** NOW!

I'VE BEEN TRAPPED ON THE CEILING! I COULDN'T DO MY HOMEWORK UP **THERE!** MY DESK IS ON THE **FLOOR!**

YOU SHOULD BE GLAD I WASN'T **OUTSIDE** WHEN IT HAPPENED, OR I'D BE SAILING THROUGH THE IONOSPHERE!

RIGHT. NOW I DON'T WANT TO HEAR ANY MORE NONSENSE UNTIL YOU'RE THROUGH WITH YOUR HOMEWORK, UNDERSTAND?

DON'T LET GO! DON'T LET GO!

IT'S... IT'S A MIRACLE! MY PERSONAL GRAVITY IS BACK TO NORMAL!

GLAD TO HEAR IT. NOW DO YOUR MATH.

YOU BET, MOM. BOY, WHAT A RELIEF TO BE PULLED DOWN INSTEAD OF UP!

I'LL CHECK YOUR PROGRESS IN A LITTLE BIT.

UH OH.

THIS HAS BEEN A MOST PECULIAR AFTERNOON.

I'VE GOT TO GET OUTSIDE BEFORE I GROW BIGGER!

I SUPPOSE I SHOULD GET MY PITUITARY GLAND CHECKED.

I KNOW! I'LL RUN DOWNTOWN AND FIND DAD AT WORK! MAYBE HE CAN HELP!

HMM... NOW WHICH BUILDING DOES DAD WORK IN? THEY ALL LOOK THE SAME.

...WELL, MAYBE DAD CAN FIND ME.

WELL? HOW'S YOUR MATH COMING ALONG?

I'VE ALMOST STARTED!

OH BROTHER! ANOTHER "DISCUSSION" ABOUT MY STUDY HABITS AND THE IMPORTANCE OF HOMEWORK.

I TRIED EXPLAINING THAT IT'S HARD TO STUDY WHEN ONE'S SIZE SUDDENLY STARTS INCREASING, BUT DOES *SHE* CARE?! HAH!

NO, IT'S JUST BLAH BLAH BLAH, LIKE IT'S ALL *MY* FAULT! MOM'S NEVER BEEN AS BIG AS A GALAXY, SO SHE CAN'T UNDERSTAND HOW ANYONE *ELSE* COULD BE! SHEEESH.

OOPS, IT LOOKS LIKE SHE'S WRAPPING UP. BETTER START NODDING.

GOOD. I'M GLAD WE HAD THIS LITTLE TALK.

DOING HOMEWORK?

YEAHHHH... BOY, YOU MISSED THE SHOW.

I GOT A BIG LECTURE FROM MOM JUST BECAUSE I GOT STUCK ON THE CEILING AND THEN GREW SO BIG I FELL OFF THE PLANET WHEN I WAS SUPPOSED TO BE DOING MY MATH!

GEE, *THAT'S* NOT VERY FAIR.

YOU SAID IT. HERE, HOW ABOUT HELPING ME HURRY UP WITH THESE PROBLEMS?

SURE! TIGERS ARE GREAT AT MATH! NOW WHAT DO THESE LITTLE HORIZONTAL LINES MEAN?

THAT'S A MINUS SIGN. LET ME KNOW WHEN YOU'RE DONE, OK? I'LL BE READING COMIC BOOKS.

CALVIN AND HOBBES by WATTERSON

OUT IN THE FARTHEST REACHES OF THE GALAXY ZOOMS INTERPLANETARY EXPLORER, *SPACEMAN SPIFF!*

OOH, NICE SCENERY!

THE MUCK MONSTERS OF MORDO ARE CLOSING IN ON OUR HERO! A FIERY FLASH OF FATALITY-FLARE MISSES BY MERE MICROMIPS!

SPIFF'S DESPERATE GAMBIT: TO FLY THROUGH THE RINGS OF PLANET ZK-5 BELOW! OUR HERO THROTTLES THE THRUSTERS AND DIVES!

SWERVING LEFT, RIGHT, UP, AND DOWN, THE AMAZING SPACEMAN SPIFF PILOTS AROUND EACH HURLING MISSILE! WHAT SKILL! WHAT FORTITU...

IT WORKS! THE MUCK MONSTERS VEER OFF, AFRAID TO FOLLOW THE FEARLESS SPIFF INTO THE FROZEN FRAGMENTS OF ICE AND ROCK!

POW! OH NO! OUR HERO IS GOING DOWN!!

Got 'im! Heh heh!

THOSE DARN LITTLE GUYS ARE HARD TO HIT, AREN'T THEY?

I HATE PLAYING "DODGE BALL" IN GYM CLASS.

WHEN ARE WE GOING TO GET A CHRISTMAS TREE?

OH, I DUNNO. PROBABLY A LITTLE AFTER NEW YEAR'S.

AFTER NEW YEAR'S?

SURE. WE CAN JUST GO UP THE STREET AND PICK THE BEST TREE FROM THE NEIGHBORS' DRIVEWAYS.

WHAT?!

SOMETIMES THERE'S STILL TINSEL ON THE TREE TOO, SO YOU DON'T EVEN HAVE TO DECORATE IT! WE'LL SAVE TIME *AND* MONEY!

OK, WHAT DID YOUR DAD TELL YOU *THIS* TIME?

YES, CALVIN? YOU HAVE A QUESTION?

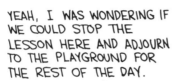

YEAH, I WAS WONDERING IF WE COULD STOP THE LESSON HERE AND ADJOURN TO THE PLAYGROUND FOR THE REST OF THE DAY.

OF COURSE NOT. NOW THEN, LET'S ALL TURN TO PAGE 24 AND...

MISS WORMWOOD?

YES?

HOW ABOUT JUST *ME* THEN?

FOR "SHOW AND TELL" TODAY, I HAVE SOMETHING THAT WILL ASTOUND AND AMAZE YOU! THIS LITTLE GUY CAN...

HAVE YOU ALL HAD YOUR SHOTS?

CALVIN AND HOBBES
by WATTERSON

DEAR SANTA,
HOW ARE YOU?

WELL, ENOUGH CHIT CHAT.
LET'S GET DOWN TO
BUSINESS.
THIS YEAR I WANT...

WILL YOU DRIVE TO WORK AND FAX MY CHRISTMAS LIST TO SANTA?

THAT'S A BIG ENVELOPE. ARE YOU MAILING A BOOK?

THIS IS MY CHRISTMAS LIST. CAN YOU BELIEVE THIS IS COSTING ME $2.40 TO SEND?

YES.

WELL, AT *THIS* PRICE, ALL I CAN SAY IS THAT SANTA HAD BETTER READ IT DARN CAREFULLY. LAST YEAR I DIDN'T GET HALF OF WHAT I WANTED.

HAVE YOU BEHAVED ANY BETTER THIS YEAR?

IT DEPENDS HOW YOU... *HEY, JUST WHAT ARE YOU INSINUATING?!* WHY, I'LL HAVE YOU KNOW I'VE BEEN A VERITABLE *ANGEL* THIS YEAR, JUST LIKE *ALWAYS!*

IN THAT CASE, WE CAN HAVE A COOKOUT WITH YOUR STOCKING CONTENTS.

DON'T GET SMART, BUB, OR I'LL WALLOP YOU ON THE 26TH.

DID YOU PUT ANYTHING ON YOUR LIST FOR *ME?*

WHAT, AND PAY MORE POSTAGE? THIS PACKAGE IS BREAKING MY ARMS ALREADY! GO WRITE YOUR *OWN* LIST!

TIDINGS OF COMFORT AND JOY TO YOU TOO.

LOOK, IT'S EVERY MAN FOR HIMSELF IN THIS WORLD. NOW GIVE ME A BOOST, WILL YA?

ARE THERE ANY MONSTERS UNDER MY BED TONIGHT?

OF COURSE NOT. COME UNDER AND SEE FOR YOURSELF.

YEAH, COME AND SEE. HEH HEH HEH.

OH RIGHT! YOU THINK I'M FALLING FOR *THAT?!* WHO AM I *TALKING* TO IF THERE AREN'T ANY MONSTERS DOWN THERE?!

UMM.. UH..

THEY'RE ALL TEETH AND DIGESTIVE TRACT. NO BRAINS AT ALL.

WHY, WE'RE DUST BALLS!

YEAH, *LITTLE* DUST BALLS!

EWW! WHAT'S *THIS* DISGUSTING STUFF?!

IT'S SPIDER PIE. YOU CAN PICK OUT THE BIG LEGS AND GIVE THEM TO YOUR DAD IF THEY'RE TOO HAIRY FOR YOU.

S-S-SPIDER P-PIE?

WHY, I BELIEVE WE'RE GOING TO HAVE A QUIET DINNER FOR ONCE.

I KNOW *I* DON'T FEEL LIKE OPENING MY MOUTH.

HEY, I *LIKE* IT!

WANT TO GO PLAY OUTSIDE?

NO, IT'S TOO MUCH TROUBLE. *FIRST* I'D HAVE TO GET UP. *THEN* I'D HAVE TO PUT ON A COAT. *THEN* I'D HAVE TO FIND MY HAT AND PUT *IT* ON. (SIGH) THEN WE'D RUN AROUND AND I'D GET TIRED, AND WHEN WE CAME IN I'D HAVE TO TAKE ALL THAT STUFF *OFF*. NO WAY.

SO WHAT ARE YOU GOING TO DO INSTEAD?

I'M JUST GOING TO SIT HERE AND WAIT FOR A GOOD TV SHOW TO COME ON.

I'LL TELL YOUR MOM TO TURN YOU TOWARD THE LIGHT AND WATER YOU PERIODICALLY.

INSTEAD OF MAKING SMART REMARKS, YOU COULD GET ME THE REMOTE CONTROL.

LOOK HOBBES, NO ONE *SAW* US FIGHTING, RIGHT? THIS CAN BE *OUR* LITTLE *SECRET*, OK? SANTA DOESN'T HAVE TO KNOW ABOUT THIS, RIGHT?

MAYBE HE DOES AND MAYBE HE DOESN'T.

OK, OK, I'LL EVEN APOLOGIZE! I'M SORRY. HOW'S THAT? SEE, IT'S OK TO FIGHT JUST A LITTLE BIT IF YOU SAY YOU'RE SORRY AFTERWARD.

YOU BIT AND KICKED.

I *SAID* I WAS SORRY! WHAT MORE DO YOU WANT?!

YOU COULD LET ME READ ALL YOUR COMIC BOOKS.

OVER MY DEAD BODY!

"DEAR SANTA, KNOW WHAT CALVIN DID TODAY?"

BOY, IF IT WASN'T SO CLOSE TO CHRISTMAS, I'D POUND YOU GOOD!

YEAH, I'D LIKE TO SEE YOU TRY!

OH NO YOU DON'T! YOU'RE NOT TEMPTING *ME!* I WANT EVERY ITEM ON MY CHRISTMAS LIST, SO I'M BEING *GOOD*. NO MATTER WHAT THE PROVOCATION!

HERE COMES SUSIE DERKINS.

REALLY? QUICK, HELP ME FIND A PINE CONE I CAN THROW AT..

..*NO!* I'M BEING *GOOD!* GOOD! GOOD! GOOD!

YOU'LL NEVER MAKE IT TILL CHRISTMAS. GIVE UP NOW AND ENJOY YOURSELF.

HI CALVIN. ARE YOU BRINGING YOUR STUFFED TIGER TO SCHOOL TODAY?

NO, HE'S JUST KEEPING ME COMPANY WHILE I WAIT FOR THE BUS.

OH.

BUT ACTUALLY, HE'S BEEN NOTHING BUT TROUBLE TODAY. HE'S TRYING TO SABOTAGE MY CHRISTMAS BY MAKING ME BE BAD INSTEAD OF GOOD.

FORTUNATELY, I ASKED SANTA FOR SUCH GREAT PRESENTS THAT I CAN WITHSTAND ANY TEMPTATION. I'M BEING AN ABSOLUTE ANGEL.

WHAT DID YOU ASK FOR?

A HEAT-SEEKING GUIDED MISSILE. I FIGURE FIVE MINUTES WITH ONE OF *THOSE* BABIES WILL MAKE UP FOR THIS WHOLE ROTTEN MONTH.

Calvin and Hobbes

by WATTERSON

'TIS THE SEASON TO ADVERTISE.

CALVIN, LOOK! YOU GOT A LETTER!

A LETTER? I DIDN'T HEAR THE MAIL TRUCK. A LETTER FOR *ME*?

THE RETURN ADDRESS SAYS "NORTH POLE".

OH MY GOSH, IT MUST BE FROM *SANTA!* SANTA SENT ME A LETTER! WOW! GEE!

READ IT! READ IT!

"DEAR CALVIN, YOU ROTTEN LITTLE KID..." OH NO!! SANTA CALLED ME *ROTTEN*! I'M DOOMED!

KEEP READING.

"I MADE A LIST, BUT I DIDN'T BOTHER CHECKING IT TWICE, BECAUSE OBVIOUSLY YOU'RE THE NAUGHTIEST KID IN THE WHOLE WORLD." AUGH!

WHAT ELSE?

"I'M WRITING TO GIVE YOU ONE LAST CHANCE. YOU'VE GOT SEVEN DAYS TO GET ON THE 'GOOD BOY' LIST." SEVEN DAYS!! OH NO! WHAT CAN I *DO?*?

MAYBE HE SAYS.

"I'D SUGGEST YOU START BY BEING KIND TO ANIMALS. PERHAPS YOU KNOW AN ANIMAL WHO WOULD LIKE A SNACK SOON. OR MAYBE YOU SHOULD LET AN ANIMAL READ YOUR COMIC BOOKS SOMETIME. THINK ABOUT IT."

SOUNDS LIKE SAGE ADVICE.

"SIGNED, SANTA CLAWS." SANTA *CLAWS?* WAIT A MINUTE! *I* RECOGNIZE THIS HANDWRITING! IT'S *YOURS!* SANTA DIDN'T WRITE THIS AT ALL!!

GIVE YOU A SNACK, HUH?! HOW ABOUT A KNUCKLE SANDWICH?!

HMPH. WELL, IT'S WHAT SANTA *WOULD'VE* WRITTEN IF HE WASN'T SO BUSY NOW.

HI DAD. I'M MAKING MY OWN NEWSPAPER TO REPORT THE EVENTS OF OUR HOUSEHOLD. WOULD YOU HELP ME OUT?

SURE, WHAT DO YOU NEED?

WELL, YOU CAN TAKE YOUR PICK. EITHER YOU CAN GIVE ME 15 BUCKS TO PAY MY LABOR AND PRODUCTION COSTS...

15 BUCKS?!

...OR YOU CAN BE THE SUBJECT OF A COMIC STRIP CALLED "DOPEY DAD."

SO IN THE NEXT PANEL, DOPEY DAD YELLS, "IT'S BEDTIME FOR YOU, YOUNG MAN!"

HEE HEE! LOOK HOW BIG I MADE HIS MOUTH!

OOH HAHH OOH HAHH

OOH HAHH OOH HAHH

OOH HAHH OOH HAHHH

I WISH WE'D GED AD AQUARIUB!

WHAT STORY WOULD YOU LIKE TONIGHT, CALVIN?

HAMSTER HUEY AND THE GOOEY KABLOOIE!

OH NO, NOT AGAIN! THAT'S WHAT YOU HEAR EVERY NIGHT! LET'S READ SOMETHING DIFFERENT.

I WANT HAMSTER HUEY! I WANT HAMSTER HUEY!

C'MON, WE'LL READ A NEW STORY TONIGHT. YOU'LL LIKE IT, I PROMISE.

NO I WON'T! I'LL STAY AWAKE UNTIL MORNING IF YOU DON'T READ HAMSTER HUEY!

I DIDN'T REMEMBER HAMSTER HUEY HAVING QUITE THAT SARCASTIC TONE OF VOICE.

OR DOING EVERYTHING SO FAST.

HA HA! IT'S CHRISTMAS! **HURRY UP, MOM AND DAD!** IT'S ALMOST DAWN!

HERE, I GOT YOU A PRESENT.

YOU GOT ME A PRESENT? GOSH HOBBES, HOW NICE!

I PICKED IT OUT MYSELF! OPEN IT!

WHY, IT'S... IT'S THREE CANS OF... UH... SALMON. UM, THANKS, HOBBES.

YOU'RE WELCOME!

GEE, I DIDN'T GET *YOU* A PRESENT. I FEEL TERRIBLE.

I THOUGHT OF THAT. SEE, YOU COULD GIVE ME MINE *BACK!* THAT WOULD BE A *GOOD* PRESENT!

WELL THEN, HERE! MERRY CHRISTMAS, HOBBES!

WHY, THANK YOU! IT'S JUST WHAT I WANTED! MERRY CHRISTMAS!

CALVIN, DID YOU KNOCK THESE CANS OVER IN THE PANTRY?

WELL, HERE WE ARE, POISED AT THE PRECIPICE OF "PALLBEARER PEAK" ON A FLIMSY, UNSTEERABLE SLED!

THE MIND RECOILS IN HORROR TO IMAGINE THE AWFUL DESCENT! YES, IT'S A THOUSAND FOOT VERTICAL DROP ONTO A BOULDER FIELD LINED WITH PRICKER BUSHES! IT'S A JOURNEY CALCULATED TO EXCEED THE HUMAN CAPACITY FOR BLINDING FEAR!

READY TO GO?

READY!

NEW HAT, DAD?

YEP.

I LIKE IT.

THANK YOU. SO DO I.

AAUGH! YOU'RE GOING TO BE LATE FOR WORK, DAD!

THIS IS THE PART OF WINTER I LIKE BEST... WHEN YOU COME INSIDE, FREEZING COLD AND SOAKED...

...AND YOU PUT ON FRESH DRY CLOTHES, AND RUN UP TO THE WARM KITCHEN, WHERE MOM'S GOT A STEAMING MUG OF HOT CHOCOLATE WAITING FOR YOU!

MOM?... MOM??
HEY MOM!

"CALVIN, I'M NEXT DOOR. DON'T HAVE ANYTHING TO EAT, OR YOU'LL SPOIL YOUR APPETITE. MOM."

IT'S GOING TO BE A LONG, COLD, DARK WINTER.

WHILE I'M DOING THIS BRAIN SURGERY, YOU CAN MAKE A DONOR AND DO A HEART TRANSPLANT!

FORGET IT, CALVIN. I'M NOT PLAYING WITH YOU ANY MORE.

calvin and Hobbes

by WATTERSON

HEE HEE HEE HEE

BUT FOR MY OWN EXAMPLE, I'D NEVER BELIEVE ONE LITTLE KID COULD HAVE SO MUCH BRAINS!

I'M A GENIUS, HOBBES. THERE'S SIMPLY NO OTHER WORD FOR IT. WHO ELSE WOULD THINK TO ARM A TOBOGGAN? IT'S JUST GENIUS!

SEE SUSIE DERKINS DOWN THERE? SHE'S BUILDING A SNOWMAN AND DOESN'T EVEN KNOW WE'RE UP HERE! WE'LL ZIP DOWN AND PELT HER SILLY WITH SNOWBALLS!

YOU STEER AND I'LL THROW! SEE, THE SNOWBALLS WILL GAIN EVEN MORE FORCE FROM OUR OWN VELOCITY! GENIUS, HUH?

HA HA! WE'LL BE A MILE AWAY BEFORE SHE CAN EVEN PICK HER HEAD OUT OF THE SNOW!

THERE SHE IS! STEER CLOSER SO I CAN GET HER! LEAN! LEAN!

AUGH! STEER! YOU'RE TOO CLOSE! MAYDAY!!

PIFF!

ANOTHER GENIUS THWARTED BY AN INCAPABLE ASSISTANT.

HEY CALVIN, LOOK UP.

CALVIN! WHAT ARE YOU DOING OUTSIDE? DIDN'T I JUST SEND YOU TO CLEAN YOUR ROOM TWO MINUTES AGO?!

NO.

I DID TOO! NOW GET BACK UPSTAIRS. I'M LOSING MY PATIENCE FOR THIS GAME!

SHE MUST'VE FOUND MY DUPLICATE! C'MON HOBBES, WE'D BETTER HURRY BEFORE HE GETS US IN MORE TROUBLE!

NUMBER THREE, HI! I'M NUMBER TWO!

CHARMED.

DUPLi

MOM SAID SHE SENT ME UPSTAIRS A MINUTE AGO! THAT MUST'VE BEEN MY DUPLICATE!

WHAT A MESS THIS IS TURNING OUT TO BE!

YOU SAID IT! *HE* GETS IN TROUBLE, BUT *I'M* THE ONE WHO GETS BLAMED! WE'D BETTER STRAIGHTEN HIM...

AAUGH!

YOUR DUPLICATOR IS A BIG SUCCESS.

OH NO!

ARE YOU KIDDING? IT BURNED OUT AFTER THE FIFTH ONE OF US!

OH NO! MY DUPLICATE MADE DUPLICATES!

HI! WE'RE NUMBERS TWO THROUGH SIX!

HI! HI! HI!

HOBBES, WHAT AM I GOING TO DO?!

BETTER TELL YOUR MOM TO PUT OUT THE EXTRA TABLE SETTINGS.

LOOK, YOU GUYS HAVE TO STAY IN HERE AND BE REAL QUIET! IF MY MOM FINDS OUT ABOUT THIS, SHE'LL HAVE A *FIT!*

STAY HERE?! NO WAY. FORGET IT.

I'M THE **ORIGINAL!** YOU HAVE TO DO WHAT I SAY!

OH YEAH? LET'S PUT IT TO A VOTE.

OK DUPLICATES, LISTEN UP. AS LONG AS YOU'RE ALL HERE AND I DON'T KNOW HOW TO GET RID OF YOU, WE MIGHT AS WELL COOPERATE.

SPECIFICALLY, WITH FIVE DUPLICATES, WE CAN DIVIDE UP THE SCHOOL WEEK SO THERE'S ONE DUPLICATE FOR EACH DAY.

IF THE REST OF US LAY LOW, WE CAN TAKE TURNS GOING TO SCHOOL, AND NO ONE WILL BE THE WISER!

GREAT!

NOW THAT STILL LEAVES US WITH THE QUESTION OF WHO GETS THE BED TONIGHT.

WE'LL FIGHT YOU FOR IT.

HI CALVIN.

I'M NOT CALVIN. I'M DUPLICATE NUMBER TWO.

WHAT ARE YOU TALKING ABOUT?

WE DREW STRAWS, AND TODAY'S MY DAY TO GO TO SCHOOL. WE'RE ALL TAKING TURNS SO WE EACH ONLY GO ONCE A WEEK.

CALVIN, YOU ARE SO WEIRD I'M NOT EVEN GOING TO TALK TO YOU.

I'M NOT CALVIN.

I WISH I LIVED SOMEPLACE WHERE I WENT TO A NORMAL BUS STOP.

ARE YOU IN CALVIN'S CLASS? WILL YOU HELP ME FIND HIS LOCKER?

CALVIN, WOULD YOU PLEASE DEMONSTRATE THE HOMEWORK PROBLEM YOU WERE ASSIGNED YESTERDAY?

I WASN'T HERE YESTERDAY.

YES, YOU WERE, CALVIN. DIDN'T YOU DO YOUR PROBLEM?

I'M NOT CALVIN. I'M DUPLICATE NUMBER FIVE. DUPLICATE *TWO* WAS HERE YESTERDAY, NOT *ME*. WE'RE ALL TAKING TURNS. NUMBER TWO WILL BE BACK NEXT WEEK, AND YOU CAN ASK HIM TO DO THE PROBLEM *THEN*.

LOOK, I DON'T SEE WHAT'S SO HARD ABOUT THIS!

WELL, HOBBES, I GUESS WE LEARNED A VALUABLE LESSON FROM THIS DUPLICATING MESS.

AND THAT IS?

AND THAT IS, UM...IT'S THAT, WELL...

OK, SO WE DIDN'T LEARN ANY BIG LESSON. SUE ME.

LIVE AND DON'T LEARN, THAT'S US.

WHAP!

DID YOU THROW THAT?!?

THROW WHAT?

LET ME SEE YOUR MITTENS! *THERE*, LOOK! FLECKS OF BARK, PIECES OF GRAVEL, SPOTS OF MUD, AND GRANULES OF ICE! THAT WAS *YOUR* SNOWBALL, ALL RIGHT!

THAT'S THE PROBLEM WITH HAVING A SIGNATURE STYLE.

HA! YOU MISSED BY A MILE! NYAH NYAHH! THBPTBH!

YES?

YOU'RE DARN LUCKY I DIDN'T GET THAT SNOW-BLOWER FOR CHRISTMAS!

CALVIN and HOBBES by WATTERSON

WHOSE BRILLIANT IDEA WAS IT TO TAKE A HIKE OUT IN THIS BITTER COLD?! HOW MUCH LONGER DO WE HAVE TO DO THIS?

I FEEL LIKE I'M IN "DR. ZHIVAGO."

ALL RIGHT, CALVIN. YOU'VE MADE YOUR POINT, I THINK.

I HATE THESE FORCED MARCHES! WHEN ARE WE GOING HOME?

THIS IS JUST A LITTLE WALK, CALVIN. THE EXERCISE IS GOOD FOR YOU.

BUT I'M *FREEZING!* IT MUST BE 80 BELOW! MY TOES ARE NUMB!

NUMB TOES BUILD CHARACTER.

YEAH? WELL, WHAT ABOUT FROSTBITE?! WHAT ABOUT HYPOTHERMIA?! WHAT ABOUT *DEATH?!* I SUPPOSE *THOSE* BUILD CHARACTER TOO! I CAN'T BELIEVE I'M OUT HERE!

THIS IS THE WORST DAY OF MY ENTIRE LIFE! I HATE THIS! AREN'T WE GOING HOME YET? IT SEEMS LIKE WE'VE BEEN WALKING FOR HOURS!

CALVIN, WILL YOU *PLEASE* STOP GRIPING?

GRIPING? *I'M* NOT GRIPING! I'M JUST *OBSERVING* WHAT A MISERABLE EXPERIENCE THIS IS! BUT OK! *SURE!* AS LONG AS I'M TRUDGING HUNDREDS OF MILES FOR NO APPARENT REASON, I MIGHT AS WELL DO IT IN *SILENCE*, RIGHT?!

JUST BECAUSE I'M OUT IN THE ELEMENTS LIKE A COMPLETE IDIOT, WATCHING MY DIGITS TURN TO ICE AND FALL OFF, I SURE AS HECK WOULDN'T EVER WANT TO SPOIL THE...

WE'RE *HOME.*

WE'RE WHAT? OH LOOK, WE'RE HOME!

WATTERSON

QUIZ:
Jack and Joe leave their homes at the same time and drive toward each other. Jack drives at 60 mph, while Joe drives at 30 mph. They pass each other in 10 minutes.

How far apart were Jack and Joe when they started?

IT WAS ANOTHER BAFFLING CASE. BUT THEN, YOU DON'T HIRE A **PRIVATE EYE** FOR THE **EASY** ONES...

I'D PLANNED TO TAKE THE DAY **OFF** AND SPEND TIME WITH A COUPLE OF **BUDDIES**. MY BUDDIES TRAVEL LIGHT AND THEY'RE FUN TO HAVE AROUND. ONE TRAVELS IN A HOLSTER, AND THE OTHER IN A HIP FLASK.

MY NAME IS **BULLET**. TRACER BULLET. WHAT PEOPLE **CALL** ME IS SOMETHING ELSE AGAIN. I'M A PRIVATE EYE. IT SAYS SO ON MY DOOR.

THE **LAST** THING I WANTED THIS MORNING WAS A **CASE** TO SOLVE, BUT THE DAME WHO BROUGHT IT WAS **PERSUASIVE**. MOST DAMES **ARE**, SOMEHOW.

GET TO WORK, CALVIN.

I TOLD HER IT WOULD COST HER FIFTY GREENBACKS A DAY, PLUS EXPENSES.

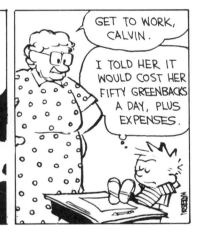

I STEPPED OUT INTO THE RAINY STREETS AND REVIEWED THE FACTS. THERE WEREN'T MANY.

TWO SAPS, JACK AND JOE, DRIVE TOWARD EACH OTHER AT 60 AND 30 MPH. AFTER 10 MINUTES, THEY PASS. I'M SUPPOSED TO FIND OUT HOW FAR APART THEY STARTED.

QUESTIONS POUR DOWN LIKE THE RAIN. WHO **ARE** THESE MUGS? WHAT WERE THEY TRYING TO ACCOMPLISH? WHY WAS JACK IN SUCH A HURRY? AND WHAT DIFFERENCE DOES IT MAKE WHERE THEY STARTED FROM??

I HAD A HUNCH THAT, BEFORE THIS WAS OVER, I'D BE SORRY I ASKED.

FIRST I FIGURED I'D TRY THE DERKINS DAME. SUSIE AND I NEVER HIT IT OFF, ALTHOUGH OCCASIONALLY WE HIT EACH OTHER.

SUSIE HAD A FACE THAT SUGGESTED SOMEBODY UPSTAIRS HAD A WEIRD SENSE OF HUMOR, BUT I WASN'T GOING TO HER PLACE FOR LAUGHS. I NEEDED INFORMATION.

THE WAY *I* LOOKED AT IT, DERKINS ACTED AWFULLY SMUG FOR A DAME WHO HAD A HEAD FOR NUMBERS AND NOT MUCH ELSE. MAYBE SHE'S GOT SOMETHING ON JACK AND JOE. THE QUESTION IS, WILL SHE SING?

NO, I WON'T TELL YOU WHAT THE ANSWER IS! DO YOUR *OWN* WORK!

THE DERKINS DAME WASN'T TALKING. SOMEONE HAD GOTTEN TO HER FIRST AND SHUT HER UP GOOD. I KNEW SUSIE, AND CLOSING HER MOUTH WOULD'VE TAKEN SOME WORK.

I NEEDED A CLUE AND A DRINK. ONE OF THEM I KNEW WHERE TO FIND.

YOU'VE MADE ENOUGH TRIPS TO THE WATER FOUNTAIN. FINISH YOUR QUIZ.

SUDDENLY A GORILLA PULLED ME IN AN ALLEY, SQUEEZED MY SPINE INTO AN ACCORDION, AND PLAYED A POLKA ON ME WITH BRASS KNUCKLES!

YOUSE AIN'T GOIN' NOWHERE, FLATFOOT.

THE INSIDE OF MY HEAD WAS EXPLODING WITH FIREWORKS. FORTUNATELY, MY LAST THOUGHT TURNED OUT THE LIGHTS WHEN IT LEFT.

WHEN I CAME TO, THE PIECES ALL FIT TOGETHER. JACK AND JOE'S LIVES WERE DEFINED BY INTEGERS. OBVIOUSLY, THEY WERE PART OF A "NUMBERS" RACKET!

BACK IN THE OFFICE, I PULLED THE FILES ON ALL THE NUMBERS *BIG* ENOUGH TO KEEP SUSIE QUIET AND WANT ME OUT OF THE PICTURE. THE ANSWER HIT ME LIKE A .44 SLUG. IT HAD TO BE THE NUMBER THEY CALLED "MR. BILLION."

Answer: 1,000,000,000

CASE CLOSED!

TIME'S UP. BRING YOUR PAPERS FORWARD.

WHAT DID YOU GET, CALVIN? I THINK THE ANSWER'S 15.

Calvin and Hobbes by WATTERSON

I THINK THIS IS MY FAVORITE TIME OF YEAR! THE NEW SNOW MAKES EVERYTHING LOOK SO PRETTY.

I THINK THIS IS MY FAVORITE TIME OF YEAR! THE NEW SNOW MUFFLES APPROACHING FOOTSTEPS! HOO HOO!

MAN, I CAN'T WAIT FOR SPRING.

Let's hurry down this hill and go home.

What's the rush?

There's a TV show on sledding I want to watch.

In my opinion, television validates existence.

Take this sled ride, for instance. The experience is fleeting and elusive. By tomorrow, we'll have forgotten it, and it may as well have not even happened.

But if we were on TV now, countless viewers would share in the event and confirm it! This ride would become a part of mass consciousness!

And on TV, the impact of an event is determined by the image, not its substance.

So with some strong visuals, our sled ride could conceivably make us cultural ICONS!

Instead of being boring ol' Calvin and Hobbes, we'd be "Calvin and Hobbes - AS SEEN ON TV"! Wouldn't that be great? Don't you wish we were on TV?

At this moment, I like my anonymity.

I think we should go for the high-brow public TV audience, don't you?

I MISSED THE BUS, MOM.

OH NO.

HURRY! IF WE JUMP IN THE CAR, YOU CAN ZOOM UP, PASS THE BUS ON A STRAIGHTAWAY, DROP ME OFF AT A LATER STOP, AND I CAN RIDE THE BUS FROM THERE!

C'MON! WHAT ARE YOU WAITING FOR? REV UP THE CAR!

MOM'S SO LAZY.

READYYY... AIMMM....

BEDTIME, KIDDO.

AW, MOM! CAN'T I WATCH THE NEXT PROGRAM?

NO, YOU NEED YOUR SLEEP. C'MON.

CAN I JUST WATCH ANOTHER 15 MINUTES? PLEASE?? OK, JUST 10 MINUTES! THEN I'LL GO STRAIGHT TO BED! FIVE MINUTES! JUST FIVE MINUTES, OK?

TURN OFF THE TV.

LOOK, I'LL JUST WATCH A FEW MORE COMMERCIALS, OK? SEE, HERE'S MY FAVORITE GUM COMMERCIAL!

I GUESS THAT GOT PRETTY PATHETIC.

calvin and hobbes
by WATTERSON

I LOVE FRESH SNOW.

IT HELPS ME AVOID CALVIN.

WINTER HAS WRAPPED THE LAND IN A SOFT, WHITE BLANKET, AND THE EARTH SLEEPS QUIETLY...

WHOAAOOMPHAA! LOOK OUT BELOW! LEAN! LEAN! AUGH!

MAYDAY! BAIL OUT! AAAAA

SMASH!

YOU CALL THAT *STEERING?* WE ALMOST GOT KILLED! *MY* FAULT? YEAH, STEP OVER *HERE* AND SAY THAT, YOU STRIPEY DOPE! THAT'S RIGHT, I'M TALKING TO *YOU!*

HEY! OW! QUIT BITING! OOF! TAKE *THAT!* OW! OW!

I THINK WHEN I GROW UP, I'LL LIVE IN THE TROPICS.

QUIT IT! QUIT IT! LET GO!

WHEE! LET'S GET THE SLED OUT OF THE TREE AND DO THAT AGAIN!

YOU KNOW WHAT WE NEED FOR OUR SLED? A SIREN!

198

HOW'S YOUR SNOW ART PROGRESSING?

I'VE MOVED INTO ABSTRACTION!

AH.

THIS PIECE IS ABOUT THE INADEQUACY OF TRADITIONAL IMAGERY AND SYMBOLS TO CONVEY MEANING IN TODAY'S WORLD.

BY ABANDONING REPRESENTATIONALISM, I'M FREE TO EXPRESS MYSELF WITH PURE FORM. SPECIFIC INTERPRETATION GIVES WAY TO A MORE VISCERAL RESPONSE.

I NOTICE YOUR OEUVRE IS MONOCHROMATIC.

WELL C'MON, IT'S JUST SNOW.

DAD, IF YOU THREW A SNOWBALL AT SOMEONE, BUT DELIBERATELY MISSED, WOULD THAT BE "BAD"?

WELL, I SUPPOSE THAT WOULD BE PROVOKING, SO YES, IT WOULD BE A LITTLE BAD.

AS BAD AS IF YOU'D HIT THE PERSON?

NO, NOT *THAT* BAD, BUT WORSE THAN IF YOU HADN'T THROWN IT AT ALL.

SUPPOSE YOU JUST *GRAZED* THE PERSON. HOW BAD WOULD *THAT* BE?

SAY MAYBE YOU KNOCKED OFF HIS HAT AND HIS GLASSES OR SOMETHING.

THAT WOULD MEAN INSTANT DEATH.

BOY, THIS PUDDING WAS GREAT! CAN I TAKE A BOWL UPSTAIRS TO HOBBES?

NO, I THINK YOU'VE HAD ENOUGH.

I DIDN'T SAY FOR *ME*. I SAID FOR *HOBBES!*

WELL, I DON'T THINK "HOBBES" NEEDS ANY EITHER.

WHY NOT?!

UM... BECAUSE TIGERS NEED TO STAY LEAN AND MEAN.

THAT'S WHAT SHE SAID.

I'M LEAN! I'M MEAN! TELL HER CHOCOLATE PUDDING MAKES MY COAT LUSTROUS.

IF THERE'S MORE TO LIFE THAN THIS, I DON'T KNOW WHAT IT IS.

140 MILLION YEARS AGO, THE INCREDIBLE 'ULTRASAURS' WANDER THE EARTH! SOME WEIGH OVER 70 TONS, AND EVEN THE VICIOUS ALLOSAURS ARE NO MATCH FOR THESE GIANTS!

BUT WAIT! A DISTANT RUMBLING SENDS THE ULTRASAURS INTO A PANICKED STAMPEDE! IS IT A VOLCANO? IS IT AN EARTHQUAKE?

NO! IT'S..IT'S A *CALVINOSAURUS!*

NAMED AFTER THE RENOWNED ARCHEOLOGIST WHO DISCOVERED IT, THE HUGE CALVINOSAUR CAN EAT AN ULTRASAUR IN A SINGLE BITE!

PHOOEY! I NEVER FIND *ANY*THING.

IT LOOKS LIKE YOU'VE HIT THE SEWER PIPE.

Panel 1: OK HOBBES, TOSS UP THIS DECK OF CARDS, AND I'LL PLUG THE ACE OF SPADES! / OH BOY, A SHOOTING TRICK!

Panel 2: GO! / BLAM BAM POW ZING BLOOIE BANG

Panel 3: HERE IT IS! WOW! SIX CLEAN HOLES THROUGH THE ACE! / PRETTY GOOD, HUH? WANT TO KNOW HOW I DID IT? I USED A HOLE PUNCHER AHEAD OF TIME!

Panel 4: HMM, ON SECOND THOUGHT, I'LL FOLD. / HEY, WHAT'S WITH THIS DECK?!

THIS MORNING I HAD A WONDERFUL DREAM. BY HOLDING MY ARMS OUT STIFF AND PUSHING DOWN HARD, I FOUND I COULD SUSPEND MYSELF A FEW FEET ABOVE THE GROUND. I FLAPPED HARDER, AND SOON I WAS SOARING EFFORTLESSLY OVER THE TREES AND TELEPHONE POLES! I COULD *FLY!* I FOLDED MY ARMS BACK AND ZOOMED LOW OVER THE NEIGHBORHOOD. EVERYONE WAS AMAZED, AND THEY RAN ALONG UNDER ME AS I SHOT BY. THEN I ROCKETED UP SO FAST THAT MY EYES WATERED FROM THE WIND. I LAUGHED AND LAUGHED, MAKING HUGE LOOPS ACROSS THE SKY! ..THAT'S WHEN MOM WOKE ME UP AND SAID I WAS GOING TO MISS THE BUS IF I DIDN'T GET MY BOTTOM OUT OF BED; 20 MINUTES LATER, HERE I AM, STANDING IN THE COLD RAIN, WAITING TO GO TO SCHOOL, AND I JUST REMEMBERED I FORGOT MY LUNCH.

TUESDAYS DON'T START MUCH WORSE THAN THIS.

I DID IT! I DID IT!

SOMEHOW I IMAGINED THIS EXPERIENCE WOULD BE MORE REWARDING.

HEWWO! IS HOBBESIE-WOBBSIE SWEEPY? OOH, HE'S JUST A BIG SNOOGIE-WOOGIE, ISN'T HE? YES HE *IS!* HEWWO, SNOOGIE-WOOGIE!

GLOMP! HEY! HEY!

OW! LEGGO, YOU BLOODTHIRSTY CARNIVORE! OW! OW! OW!

I CAN SEE WHY LITTLE TABBY CATS ARE SO MUCH MORE POPULAR.

ONCE UPON A TIME, THERE WAS A... HOLD IT.

YOU KNOW WHAT *ID* LIKE TO SEE? I'D LIKE TO SEE THE THREE BEARS EAT THE THREE LITTLE PIGS, AND THEN THE BEARS JOIN UP WITH THE BIG BAD WOLF AND EAT GOLDILOCKS AND LITTLE RED RIDING HOOD!

TELL ME A STORY LIKE *THAT*, OK?

AND HOW SHOULD HANSEL AND GRETEL MEET *THEIR* UNTIMELY DEMISE?

THE WITCH EATS THEM AND THEN THE WOLF EATS THE WITCH.

HEY DAD, CAN I TAKE THE GAS CAN FOR THE LAWN MOWER OUT IN THE BACK YARD?

WHAT ON EARTH FOR? IT'S 8:00 AT NIGHT!

I WANT TO POUR GASOLINE IN BIG LETTERS ON THE LAWN...

" AND SET FIRE TO IT SO AIRPLANES CAN READ IT AS THEY FLY OVER!

NO, YOU CAN'T DO THAT! DON'T BE RIDICULOUS!

I DON'T EVEN WANT TO KNOW WHAT HE INTENDED TO WRITE.

Calvin and Hobbes
by WATTERSON

BEWARE! FALLING BUCKEYES

HERE COMES SOMEBODY!

THIS MEETING OF THE TOP SECRET CLUB G.R.O.S.S. (*GET RID OF SLIMY GIRLS*) WILL COME TO ORDER. TODAY THIS AUGUST ASSEMBLY WILL DECIDE WHETHER TO DEMOTE PRESIDENT HOBBES ON CHARGES OF HERESY!

HERESY?!

LET THE RECORD SHOW THAT THE DEFENDANT MADE AN *UN*DISPARAGING COMMENT ABOUT THE POSSIBLE MEMBERSHIP OF SUSIE DERKINS, AN ADMITTED GIRL AND ENEMY OF THIS CLUB.

LET THE RECORD *ALSO* SHOW THAT SUPREME DICTATOR-FOR-LIFE CALVIN IS A NINCOMPOOP.

OK, JUST FOR *THAT*, YOU'RE ALSO CHARGED WITH INSUBORDINATION! THIS COURT FINDS YOU GUILTY ON BOTH COUNTS AND STRIPS YOU OF YOUR TITLE!

HA! AS COURT STENOGRAPHER, I REFUSE TO ENTER THE VERDICT! IN FACT, I'M **PRO-MOTING** MYSELF TO "EL TIGRE NUMERO UNO"!

OH YEAH?! WELL THEN, I PROMOTE *MY*SELF TO "MOST HIGHEST, GRANDEST, EXALTED, UM, SUPREME, UH.."

THERE! I WROTE "HOBBES EQUALS GREAT" IN THE OFFICIAL CLUB NOTEBOOK! NOW IT'S A LAW!

IT IS NOT! GIMME THAT!

HOBS = GRAT

HA HA HA! *I'M* WRITING "HOBBES EQUALS UGLY FUR BALL"! WHAT DO YOU THINK OF *THAT*?

OH HO! I TAKE THE SUPREME DICTATOR HAT! NOW *I'M* THE SUPREME DICTATOR!

YOU GIVE THAT BACK!

I DECLARE YOU NULL AND VOID!

TRUCE?

TRUCE.

WHAT A GREAT CLUB. TOO BAD WE DON'T HAVE MORE MEMBERS.

MAYBE WE SHOULD ALLOW SUSIE TO JOIN.

DO YOU... I MEAN, DOES *HOBBES* WANT ANY TUNA FISH THIS WEEK?

NO, HOBBES STOPPED EATING CANNED TUNA. YOU KNOW, THEY KILL DOLPHINS TO GET IT.

OK, I'LL PUT IT BACK.

SO WHAT DOES HOBBES LIKE NOW INSTEAD?

FRESH SWORDFISH STEAKS. HE LIKES THEM GRILLED OUTSIDE.

MM-HMM. HOW ABOUT PEANUT BUTTER?

HERE'S SOME CLEAN CLOTHES. WILL YOU PUT THEM AWAY PLEASE?

HEY, MY UNDERWEAR ISN'T PRESSED! NEITHER ARE MY SOCKS! YOU DIDN'T FINISH IRONING!

BUDDY, IF YOU WANT YOUR UNDERWEAR IRONED, YOU CAN DO IT YOURSELF!

WHAT KIND OF MOTHER *ARE* YOU?!

SHE SHOULD TAKE MORE PRIDE IN HER WORK.

I ASKED MOM IF I WAS A GIFTED CHILD. ...SHE SAID THEY CERTAINLY WOULDN'T HAVE *PAID* FOR ME.

YOU CAN RELATE THIS LITTLE STORY WHEN THE REPORTERS ASK HOW I WENT BAD.

MOM! HOBBES IS READING MY COMIC BOOKS! TELL HIM TO STOP!

I TOLD HIM TO GO BUY HIS OWN, AND HE *SNARLED* AT ME! MAKE HIM GIVE 'EM BACK!

MAYBE YOU SHOULD BE GLAD HE'S MORE LITERATE THAN MOST STUFFED ANIMALS.

BUT THEY'RE *MY* COMIC BOOKS, NOT *HIS*!

WELL, YOU SHOULD LEARN TO SHARE. I DON'T THINK HOBBES WILL HURT THEM.

ARE YOU KIDDING?! HE DREW A MUSTACHE AND GLASSES ON EVERY PICTURE OF NUKE-MAN LAST ISSUE! IN *PEN*!

WHY DON'T YOU GO PLAY OUTSIDE, CALVIN.

HOW'S YOUR MATH COMING?

I DON'T *DO* MATH ANY MORE. I DECIDED I'M MORE OF A "VISUAL" PERSON.

GOOD. VISUALIZE BEING THE ONLY 45-YEAR-OLD IN FIRST GRADE.

VISUALIZING A FEW SUMS NOW, EH?

ACTUALLY, I'M VISUALIZING *YOU* IN TRACTION. HELP ME DO THESE, OK?

HEY HOBBES, I'LL GIVE YOU 20 QUESTIONS TO GUESS WHAT I HAVE IN MY HANDS, OK?

OK. IS IT LOATHSOME?

YES!

IS IT SOME BIG CENTIPEDE WITH POISON PINCHERS?

CENTIPEDES HAVE POISON PINCHERS?

I THINK SO.

MAN, IT'S A GOOD THING YOU GUESSED IT SO FAST!

WITH YOU, IT'S NEVER TOO DIFFICULT.

WHERE DO WE KEEP THE EXTENSION CORDS?

IN THE PANTRY, ON THE BOTTOM SHELF.

WHERE DO WE KEEP THE BLADES FOR DAD'S ELECTRIC SAW?

IN THE... WHY DO YOU WANT TO KNOW?

HUH? OH, I'M JUST MAKING AN INVENTORY LIST SO WE'LL ALWAYS KNOW WHERE TO FIND THINGS.

I GET THE FEELING THERE WAS NO RIGHT ANSWER TO THAT QUESTION.

CALVIN, COME OUT FROM WHEREVER YOU'RE HIDING AND TAKE YOUR BATH!

DO YOU HEAR ME, CALVIN?! I MEAN NOW!

OH NO! LOOK AT YOU! AUGH! GET OFF THE RUG!

LIKE IT'S MY FAULT SHE HASN'T GOTTEN THE CHIMNEY SWEPT.

MOM! MOM! I JUST SAW THE FIRST ROBIN OF SPRING! CALL THE NEWSPAPER QUICK!

HA HA! A FRONT PAGE WRITE-UP! A COMMEMORATIVE PLAQUE! A CIVIC CEREMONY! ALL FOR ME! HOORAY! HOORAY!

OH BOY! SHOULD I PUT THE PRIZE MONEY IN A TRUST FUND, OR BLOW IT ALL AT ONCE? HA HA! I CAN'T BELIEVE I DID IT!

CALVIN...

IT'S A HARD, BITTER, CRUEL WORLD TO HAVE TO GROW UP IN, HOBBES.

CHEER UP! DID I TELL YOU I SAW A ROBIN YESTERDAY?

THERE GOES ROSALYN AROUND THE HOUSE AGAIN. SHE STILL DOESN'T KNOW YOU SNEAKED BACK INSIDE.

NOW I'LL CHANGE BACK INTO MY SECRET IDENTITY ALTER EGO!

UH OH. SHE SAW THE LIGHT ON IN THIS ROOM. SHE'S COMING IN!

QUICK! GET IN THE COVERS! PRETEND WE'VE JUST BEEN READING IN BED!

BUT SHE KNOWS YOU ATTACKED HER AND RAN OUTSIDE HALF AN HOUR AGO!

THAT WAS *STUPENDOUS MAN*, NOT MILD-MANNERED CALVIN! *I'VE* BEEN IN BED WITH MY PJs ON SINCE 8:00.

YOU THINK SHE'S GOING TO BELIEVE *THAT*?

MY COVERS ARE *HERE*. MY PAJAMAS ARE *HERE*. IT'S AS PLAIN AS CAN BE!

ALL RIGHT! *I* FOUND YOU!

FOUND?? WHY, WHAT DO YOU MEAN? I'VE BEEN IN BED READING ALL EVENING WITH HOBBES.

DON'T GIVE ME THAT! YOU JUST NOW SNEAKED INSIDE, TOOK OFF YOUR SILLY COSTUME, AND JUMPED IN BED! I KNOW WHAT YOU DID! WELL YOU'RE GONNA GET IT *NOW*, BUCKO!

OH YEAH? WHAT ARE YOU GOING TO DO TO ME, HUH? YOU CAN'T SEND ME TO BED WHEN I'M ALREADY *IN* BED! SORRY TO SPOIL YOUR FUN, YOU EEL!

OK, DOWNSTAIRS! *MARCH!*

HEY, YOU CAN'T TAKE ME *OUT* OF BED! I NEED MY *SLEEP!* HEY! HEY!

WHILE YOUR DAD IS TAKING ROSALYN HOME, PERHAPS *YOU'D* LIKE TO EXPLAIN WHAT HAPPENED TONIGHT.

GOSH MOM, WHAT'S TO TELL? AT 8:00, I PUT ON MY PAJAMAS, BRUSHED MY TEETH AND WENT STRAIGHT TO BED. NOTHING HAPPENED.

AND THIS?

UH... *LIES!* ALL LIES! ROSALYN MADE ME DO THAT JUST SO I'D GET IN TROUBLE! SHE HATES KIDS! NONE OF THAT IS TRUE! I WENT STRAIGHT TO BED!

NICE TRY, PINOCCHIO.

WELL WHO WOULD'VE THOUGHT ROSALYN WOULD MAKE ME WRITE A FULL CONFESSION?!

HMPH! —

LIFE'S DISAPPOINTMENTS ARE HARDER TO TAKE WHEN YOU DON'T KNOW ANY SWEAR WORDS.

BOY, I'M IN A ROTTEN MOOD. THE WORLD HAD JUST BETTER LOOK OUT!

HEY YOU, YOU'RE IN MY WAY! MOVE IT!

WHAT'S THE MATTER? DID YOU GO DEAF?! GET OUT OF MY WAY! SCRAM!

C'MON, HURRY UP! YOU THINK I'VE GOT ALL DAY?!

NOW ARE YOU GOING TO STEP ASIDE, OR *WHAT*?! I'M COMING THROUGH!

MMPH! GGGHH! WHAT ARE YOU DOING?! I *SAID* MOVE ASIDE!!

DOGGONE IT, WHEN I SAY *MOVE*, I EXPECT YOU TO JUMP! *MOVE!*

MOVE! MOVE! MOVE! MOVE! MOVE!

HEY! PUT ME DOWN! WHERE ARE YOU TAKING ME?! I DEMAND AN EXPLANA... HEY, IS THAT A MUD HOLE?! YOU'D BETTER NOT! YOU HEAR ME?!

SEE WHY I'M IN SUCH A BAD MOOD?!

NO TV FOR A WEEK! WHAT INJUSTICE!

THEY THINK THEY'VE WON, BUT THEY HAVEN'T!

I'LL SHOW 'EM! I *REFUSE* TO LEARN A LESSON!

I'M INDOMITABLE! THEY CAN'T CHANGE ME!

I'LL SIT IN FRONT OF THE TV ALL WEEK, EVEN IF I CAN'T TURN IT ON!

DAD, WILL YOU EXPLAIN THE THEORY OF RELATIVITY TO ME? I DON'T UNDERSTAND WHY TIME GOES SLOWER AT GREAT SPEED.

IT'S BECAUSE YOU KEEP CHANGING TIME ZONES. SEE, IF YOU FLY TO CALIFORNIA, YOU GAIN THREE HOURS ON A FIVE-HOUR FLIGHT, RIGHT?

SO IF YOU GO AT THE SPEED OF LIGHT, YOU GAIN *MORE* TIME, BECAUSE IT DOESN'T TAKE AS LONG TO GET THERE. OF COURSE, THE THEORY OF RELATIVITY ONLY WORKS IF YOU'RE GOING WEST.

GEE, THAT'S NOT WHAT MOM SAID AT **ALL**! SHE MUST BE TOTALLY OFF HER ROCKER.

WELL, WE MEN ARE BETTER AT ABSTRACT REASONING. GO TELL HER THAT.

MOM, CAN WE GO OUT TO THE HIGHWAY?

DO WHAT?

SEE, I'LL PUT ON MY ROLLER SKATES AND TIE A ROPE FROM THE CAR BUMPER TO MY WAIST. THEN WHEN I GIVE YOU THE HIGH FIVE, YOU PATCH OUT WHILE I RIDE BEHIND AT 55 MPH!

WHAT DO YOU SAY? CAN WE GO?

I SURE WISH *YOU* COULD DRIVE.

WOW! NOBODY IS ON THE SWINGS! I CAN'T BELIEVE IT!

HA HA! I ALMOST *NEVER* GET A SWING AT RECESS!

THIS IS GREAT!

NO ONE IS TELLING ME TO HURRY UP!

HIGHER! HIGHER!

WHEE!

..EITHER THIS IS MY LUCKY DAY, OR I MISSED THE END-OF-RECESS BELL AGAIN.

HEY CALVIN, DIDN'T YOU SIGN UP TO PLAY BASEBALL AT RECESS?

NO, WHY?

YOU MUST BE THE ONLY BOY WHO DIDN'T. ALL THE OTHERS ARE PLAYING IN THE BACK FIELDS.

YOU MEAN I'M THE ONLY BOY ON A PLAYGROUND FULL OF *GIRLS*.?.!

IT SURE LOOKS LIKE IT. WANT TO RIDE ON THE TEETER-TOTTER WITH ME?

OH NO! I'M IN *COOTIE CENTRAL*! I HAVEN'T HAD MY SHOTS!

RELAX. STUPIDITY PRODUCES ANTIBODIES.

AIR FILTER! AIR FILTER!

WHY DIDN'T YOU SIGN UP TO PLAY BASE-BALL LIKE THE REST OF THE BOYS? DON'T YOU LIKE SPORTS?

I DUNNO. I'D JUST RATHER RUN AROUND.

I HATE ALL THE RULES AND ORGANIZATION AND TEAMS AND RANKS IN SPORTS.

SOMEBODY'S ALWAYS YELLING AT YOU, TELLING YOU WHERE TO BE, WHAT TO DO, AND WHEN TO DO IT.

I FIGURE WHEN I WANT *THAT*, I'LL JOIN THE ARMY AND AT LEAST GET PAID.

Hey, lookit the sissy who didn't sign up for recess baseball!

I'M NOT A SISSY!

Oh yeah? You'd rather play dolls on the playground with girls.

I WASN'T PLAYING WITH DOLLS!

Sure you weren't! Let me see your Barbie doll, you sissy wimp!

I'M NOT A WIMP! IN FACT, I WAS GOING TO THE OFFICE TO SIGN UP FOR BASEBALL RIGHT NOW!

THEN AGAIN, IF I'M NOT A WIMP, WHY AM I TAKING THE PATH OF LEAST RESISTANCE?

OFFICE

I SIGNED UP TO PLAY BASEBALL EVERY RECESS, AND I DON'T EVEN *LIKE* BASEBALL THAT MUCH.

I MEAN, IT'S FUN PLAYING BASEBALL WITH JUST *YOU*, BECAUSE WE BOTH GET TO PITCH, BAT, RUN AND CATCH ALL AT ONCE. WE GET TO *DO* EVERYTHING.

MOSTLY WE JUST ARGUE OVER THE RULES WE MAKE UP! THAT'S THE PART *I* LIKE!

BUT THIS WILL BE WITH *TEAMS* AND ASSIGNED POSITIONS AND AN UMPIRE! IT'S *BORING* PLAYING IT THE *REAL* WAY!

DO YOU EVEN KNOW *HOW* TO PLAY THE REAL WAY?

SEE, THAT'S *ANOTHER* PROBLEM! SUPPOSE THEY MAKE ME A HALFBACK. CAN I TACKLE THE SHORTSTOP OR NOT?

I HEAR YOU SIGNED UP TO PLAY SOFTBALL AT RECESS.

YEAH, BUT I DIDN'T EVEN WANT TO. I JUST DID IT TO STOP GETTING TEASED.

WELL, SPORTS ARE GOOD FOR YOU. THEY TEACH TEAMWORK AND COOPERATION. YOU LEARN HOW TO WIN GRACIOUSLY AND ACCEPT DEFEAT. IT BUILDS CHARACTER.

EVERY TIME I'VE BUILT CHARACTER, I'VE REGRETTED IT! I DON'T *WANT* TO LEARN TEAMWORK! I DON'T *WANT* TO LEARN ABOUT WINNING AND LOSING! HECK, I DON'T EVEN WANT TO *COMPETE!* WHAT'S WRONG WITH JUST HAVING FUN BY YOURSELF, HUH?!

WHEN YOU GROW UP, IT'S NOT ALLOWED.

ALL THE MORE REASON I SHOULD DO IT *NOW!*

C'MON, LET'S GO OUTSIDE AND TRY SOME CATCHES BEFORE DINNER, OK? A LITTLE PRACTICE WILL MAKE YOU MORE CONFIDENT TOMORROW AT RECESS.

I HATE THESE FATHER-SON THINGS.

GO OUT A LITTLE BIT, AND I'LL HIT YOU A GROUNDER.

WHY DID I SIGN UP FOR THIS? I SHOULD JUST MOVE.

READY? NOW, BE SURE TO RUN UP TO THE BALL. DON'T JUST LET IT ROLL TO YOU.

ARE YOU OK? SOMETIMES THE BALL BOUNCES UP LIKE THAT, AND YOU'VE GOT TO BE READY.

THAGS FOR THE TIB, DAD. FIDE MY NODE AND PUD ID IN ICE SO THEY CAN SEW ID BAG OD!

GOODNESS, WHAT HAPPENED?! YOU WERE ONLY OUT THERE A MINUTE!

A GROUNDER BOUNCED UP AND HIT CALVIN IN THE NOSE.

I'B BLEEDIG! BY ODE DAD ID TRYIG TO GILL ME!

HOLD YOUR HEAD BACK, HONEY. HERE'S SOME MORE TISSUES.

I'B NOD PLAYIG BADEBALL EDDY MORE! NEBBER AGAIN! I HADE IT!

SIT STILL SO THE BLEEDING CAN STOP, OK?

I GUESS WE CAN FORGET HAVING A MILLIONAIRE BASEBALL PLAYER SUPPORT US IN OUR OLD AGE.

DEAR!

ALL BY CHARAGDER ID DRIPPIG OUT BY NODE!

HOW'S THE NOSE?

IT FINALLY STOPPED BLEEDING. I GUESS THAT MEANS I'LL HAVE TO GO TO SCHOOL TOMORROW.

MY WHOLE LIFE IS A DISASTER. I GET INJURED JUST TRYING TO LEARN THE SKILLS IT TAKES TO PLAY A GAME I DON'T EVEN WANT TO PLAY!

YOUR NOSE IS PROBABLY ALL CLOGGED UP NOW, HUH?

SNRKK YEAH, WHY?

IF YOU SNORE, I'M TILTING THE BED SO YOU ROLL OUT THE WINDOW.

IT'S ALWAYS NICE TO HAVE A SYMPATHETIC FRIEND TO TALK TO.

I SEE YOU'RE BRINGING A GLOVE TODAY. DID YOU SIGN UP FOR RECESS BASEBALL?

YEAH, DON'T REMIND ME.

YOU'RE LUCKY THAT *GIRLS* DON'T HAVE TO PUT UP WITH THIS NONSENSE. IF A *GIRL* DOESN'T WANT TO PLAY SPORTS, THAT'S FINE!

BUT IF A *GUY* DOESN'T SPEND HIS AFTERNOONS CHASING SOME STUPID BALL, HE'S CALLED A WIMP! YOU GIRLS HAVE IT EASY!

ON THE OTHER HAND, *BOYS* AREN'T EXPECTED TO SPEND THEIR LIVES 20 POUNDS UNDERWEIGHT.

AND IF YOU DON'T PLAY SPORTS, YOU DON'T GET TO MAKE BEER COMMERCIALS!

MR. LOCKJAW? I'M CALVIN. I'M SUPPOSED TO BE ON TEAM FIVE NOW.

OH YES, YOU'RE THE ONE WHO SIGNED UP LATE. HMM... OK, YOU GO PLAY LEFT FIELD.

LEFT FIELD. OK, I KNOW THAT. LET'S SEE, IF I'M *HERE*, THEN LEFT FIELD WOULD BE...

THAT WAY. PLAY *DEEP* LEFT FIELD.

I GUESS THIS IS PRETTY DEEP.

I THINK BASEBALL IS THE MOST BORING GAME IN THE WORLD. I'VE BEEN STANDING OUT HERE IN DEEP LEFT FIELD ALL THIS TIME, AND NOT A SINGLE BALL HAS COME OUT HERE!

ACTUALLY, I SUPPOSE THAT'S JUST AS WELL. I DON'T KNOW WHAT BASE TO THROW TO ANYWAY. IN FACT, I'M NOT EVEN SURE I CAN THROW THAT FAR.

HEY, WHAT'S EVERYONE DOING? ARE PEOPLE SWITCHING TEAMS, OR WHAT? THE GUYS AT BAT ARE NOW OUT *HERE!*

WELL, I'M SURE SOMEONE WOULD TELL ME IF I WAS SUPPOSED TO BE DOING ANYTHING DIFFERENT.

OUR HERO, THE FEARLESS SPACEMAN SPIFF, IS MAROONED ON THE MOST DISTANT PLANET IN THE GALAXY!

THERE'S NO HOPE OF RESCUE FROM THIS BLEAK AND ISOLATED WORLD!

OH, WHAT A DESOLATE PLACE TO BE TRAPPED! SPIFF TRIES DESPERATELY TO REPAIR HIS DISABLED SPACECRAFT!

CRACK

HIGH FLY TO LEFT FIELD! WHO'S OUT THERE?!

OUR HERO PAUSES. THERE'S SOME COMMOTION ON THE HORIZON. *ALIENS!* SPIFF GRABS HIS BLASTER!

WHERE'S THE LEFT FIELDER?!

SOMEBODY CATCH IT!

LEFT FIELD?! HEY, THAT'S *ME!*

WOW! A HIGH FLY RIGHT TO ME! I GOT IT! I GOT IT!

I CAUGHT IT!!

HE CAUGHT IT! IT'S AN OUT!

WAP!

I'M JUST A NATURAL ATHLETE, I GUESS.

HEY, WHO'S *HE?*

ISN'T HE ON THE OTHER TEAM?

HEY, LOOK WHO MADE THE OUT!

IT'S *CALVIN!*

HECK, IT WAS NOTHING, GUYS. WHEN YOU'RE IN TOP PHYSICAL CONDITION LIKE ME, YOU CAN...

YOU MORON! WHAT WERE YOU DOING IN THE OUTFIELD?! IT'S A NEW INNING! WE'RE UP TO *BAT!*

HUH?

YOU CAUGHT THE BALL FOR THE WRONG TEAM! YOU GOT OUR OWN GUY OUT! WHAT A DWEEB! WHAT A JERK! WHAT AN *IDIOT!*

OOPS, I DROPPED THE CATCH. IT DOESN'T COUNT NOW, RIGHT?

GET HIM OFF OUR TEAM, MR. LOCKJAW!

CAN I HIT HIM WITH THE BAT? PLEASE? PLEASE??

TODAY FOR "SHOW AND TELL," I HAVE A SOUVENIR FROM THE AFTERLIFE! YES, YOU HEARD RIGHT! EQUALLY AMAZING IS MY OWN STORY OF YESTERDAY AFTERNOON, WHEN I ACTUALLY DIED OF BOREDOM!

I WAS DOING MY HOMEWORK, WHEN SUDDENLY I COLLAPSED! I FELT MYSELF RISING, AND I COULD SEE MY CRUMPLED BODY ON THE FLOOR. I DRIFTED UP IN A SHAFT OF LIGHT AND I ENTERED THE NEXT WORLD!

EVENTUALLY, MY HEART STARTED AGAIN AND I CAME BACK TO LIFE... BUT NOT BEFORE BRINGING THIS BACK!

A YO-YO?

IT WAS PRETTY BORING THERE, TOO.

LET'S HAVE A LOOK AT THAT HOMEWORK.

AND SO, HAVING EATEN HER FILL, THE MOTHER BIRD RETURNS TO HER NEST...

...WHERE SHE REGURGITATES THE WORMS TO FEED HER HUNGRY BROOD.

...SIGHHHHHH...

CALVIN, PAY ATTENTION!

AUGH

THERE'S NO HEAD REST ON THIS CHAIR! I SHOULD SUE FOR WHIPLASH!

Calvin and Hobbes
by WATTERSON

ARE YOU GOING TO READ CALVIN A STORY?

ONLY IF IT'S NOT THAT AWFUL "HAMSTER HUEY AND THE GOOEY KABLOOIE".

OH, BUT YOU LOOK SO *CUTE* DOING THE "HAPPY HAMSTER HOP"!

I DON'T *WANT* TO LOOK CUTE!!

WHAT STORY WOULD YOU LIKE TONIGHT, CALVIN?

I WANT A STORY ABOUT HOBBES AND ME.

OK...HMM.. LET'S SEE... ONCE THERE WAS A BOY NAMED CALVIN WHO LIVED WITH A TIGER NAMED HOBBES.

THIS IS GREAT!

TODAY THEY GOT UP AT THE CRACK OF DAWN AND MADE A HUGE RUCKUS RUNNING *UP* THE STAIRS, GALUMP, GALUMP, GALUMP, AND SLIDING *DOWN* AGAIN, BUMP, BUMP BUMP, BUMP.'

YEAH, THEN THE *BIG BAD DAD* YELLED THAT IF WE DIDN'T KNOCK IT OFF, HE'D MAIL US TO *PLUTO* THIRD CLASS!

WHO'S TELLING THIS STORY, YOU OR ME?

YOU *DID* SAY THAT! DON'T TRY TO DENY IT!

SO FINALLY, CALVIN GOT THE HINT AND HE WENT TO ROT HIS INNARDS WITH CHOCOLATE CEREAL, AND TO ROT HIS BRAIN WATCHING CARTOONS.

HEY! *NO* EDITORIALS!

AT LAST CALVIN AND HOBBES WENT OUTSIDE, AND IT WAS NICE AND QUIET IN THE HOUSE AGAIN. AT LEAST FOR A WHILE. WELL, GOOD NIGHT!

GOOD NIGHT:? THAT'S NOT THE END! YOU DIDN'T EVEN GET US TO LUNCHTIME!

THAT'S RIGHT... IT'S NOT THE END OF THE STORY. THIS STORY DOESN'T *HAVE* AN END. YOU AND HOBBES WILL WRITE MORE OF IT TOMORROW AND EVERY DAY AFTER. BUT NOW IT'S TIME TO SLEEP, SO GOOD NIGHT.

OH! OK, GOOD NIGHT.

THIS *IS* A GOOD STORY ABOUT US IF IT DOESN'T END! THAT'S THE KIND OF STORY I LIKE BEST! GOOD NIGHT, OL' BUDDY!

ME TOO! SEE YOU TOMORROW!

CALVIN and HOBBES by WATTERSON

I'M *FREEEEEEEEEEEEEEEEEEEEE*

HO HO! THEY *TRIED* TO MAKE ME LEARN, BUT *I* WAS TOO *TOUGH* FOR 'EM!

I'M HOME!

WHY HELLO, CALVIN! DO COME IN, WON'T YOU?

CLICK.

HEY! HEY!

MAY I READ ALL YOUR COMIC BOOKS? I *MAY*? THANK YOU, CALVIN!

MAY I DRAW MUSTACHES ON ALL THE SUPERHEROES? I *MAY*? OH JOY!

I'LL GET HIM FOR THIS IF IT TAKES MY WHOLE LIFE.

I'VE COME UP WITH A NEW SYSTEM FOR DOING HOME-WORK. I CALL IT "EFFECTIVE TIME MANAGEMENT," OR "ETM" FOR SHORT.

I'VE DRAWN UP A SCHEDULE FOR EACH SCHOOL SUBJECT, AND I USE THIS KITCHEN TIMER TO MONITOR MY PACE.

THANKS TO ETM, I'M MUCH MORE EFFICIENT, AND MY WORK GOES FASTER!

RINGG

THERE! MY MATH MINUTE IS UP! SET THE CLOCK FOR MY SPELLING ASSIGNMENT, OK?

UM, YOUR SCHEDULE CALLS FOR SMALLER TIME INCREMENTS THAN THIS CLOCK CAN MEASURE.

NO I WON'T TAKE A PICTURE OF YOU.

KA

ZAM!

WHAT?

CALVIN and HOBBES

by WATTERSON

TOAD STROGANOFF!

..EWWWW..

POKE POKE

AUGH!

CLINK
CLINK
CLINK

HA!

SPLORPP!

SPLAT!

DON'T BLAME *ME*. I'M THE ONE WHO SAID WE SHOULD CALL FOR A PIZZA.

EWW! WHAT **IS** THIS?! IT LOOKS LIKE **COMPOST!**

MOM DOESN'T APPRECIATE ME.

HEY HOBBES, WHAT'S A "PAPER TIGER"?

IT'S LIKE A PAPER BOY. YOU KNOW, A TIGER WITH A NEWSPAPER ROUTE.

OH.

THIS BOOK MAKES NO SENSE AT ALL.

HEY DAD, WOULD YOU PAY ME A DOLLAR TO EAT A BUG?

NO, YOU'D HAVE TO EAT A BUCKET OF BUGS BEFORE I'D PAY YOU A DOLLAR.

A WHOLE BUCKET?

OR I'D PAY YOU A DOLLAR TO PICK UP STICKS IN THE BACK YARD.

ALL MY **REAL** SKILLS ARE UNDERVALUED.

ON DISTANT PLANET ZARK, WE FIND THE EMPTY RED SPACECRAFT OF OUR HERO, THE BOLD *SPACEMAN SPIFF!*

UH OH! UP AHEAD, THE ROCKS ARE CHARRED WITH DEATH RAY BLASTS! A VIOLENT STRUGGLE TOOK PLACE HERE!

AND ONLY THE TRACKS OF A LARGE, SINISTER ALIEN LEAVE THE SCENE! WHAT HAS HAPPENED TO THE EARTHLING EXPLORER?

CALVIN, THIS IS HUMILIATING!!

I DON'T WANT TO GO! PUT ME DOWN!

SPACEMAN SPIFF IS BEING HELD PRISONER BY HIDEOUS ALIENS! WHAT DO THEY WANT WITH HIM?

SPIFF IS SOON TO FIND OUT! OUR HERO IS CALLED BEFORE THE ALIEN POTENTATE!

..WHERE IT BECOMES CLEAR THAT SPIFF IS ABOUT TO BE *SACRIFICED...*

..TO APPEASE THE EVIL GOD THEY CALL "NOLLIJ"!

UP TO THE BLACKBOARD. HURRY UP.

STARING DEATH IN THE FACE, OUR HERO THINKS FAST.

11 - 4 =

INCHING CLOSER TO THE SACRIFICIAL PIT, SPIFF SLOWLY AND SMOOTHLY REACHES FOR THE TINY ATOM BLASTER CONCEALED IN HIS BELT!

YAA! ALL RIGHT, YOU BLOODSUCKING, MUTANT CHROMOSOMAL DISASTERS! NOBODY MOVE! I'M OUTTA HERE!

CALVIN, GIVE ME THAT RUBBER BAND RIGHT THIS MINUTE!

I SAID NOBODY MOVE!

SPIFF ESCAPES! THE DANK AND SMELLY CORRIDORS OF THE ALIEN FORTRESS ARE DESERTED! ALL THE ALIENS HAD GATHERED FOR THE SPECTACLE OF OUR HERO'S DEMISE!

THE FEARLESS SPACE EXPLORER MAKES IT TO THE PLANET SURFACE, BUT THE ALIEN QUEEN IS IN PURSUIT!

CALVIN, GET BACK HERE!

SPIFF JUMPS INTO THE COCKPIT, PRESSURIZES THE LAUNCH THRUSTERS, AND...

BLASTS OFF! OUR HERO IS SAFE!

Tomorrow: OR IS HE ??

CALVIN! WHAT ARE YOU DOING HOME?! IT'S NOT EVEN NOON!

UH, THEY LET US OUT EARLY TODAY. THERE WAS, UM, A GAS LEAK.

WHAT?! DOES ANYONE KNOW YOU LEFT?! I'M CALLING THE SCHOOL.

DON'T WASTE YOUR TIME! EVERYONE WAS EVACUATED! THERE'S NOBODY THERE!

HELLO? ELEMENTARY SCHOOL OFFICE, PLEASE.

OUR HERO HADN'T COUNTED ON RUNNING INTO A ZARK ENFORCER SHIP! SPIFF'S EVASIVE MANEUVERS COME TO NAUGHT! THIS COULD BE THE END!

BOY, I SURE GOT IN BIG TROUBLE TODAY! MOM HIT THE ROOF WHEN SHE FOUND OUT I JUST LEFT SCHOOL.

WHAT HAPPENED?

SHE DROVE ME BACK AND WE HAD TO TALK TO MY TEACHER AND THE PRINCIPAL! THEY TALKED ABOUT MY STUDY HABITS, AND NOW I'VE GOT EXTRA HOMEWORK!

OOH.

AND DAD IS GOING TO CHECK IT EVERY NIGHT TO MAKE SURE IT'S DONE RIGHT! CAN YOU BELIEVE IT?!

SO TRY TO DO AN EXTRA GOOD JOB NOW, OK?

YOU'RE LUCKY TIGERS ARE SO SMART.

CALVIN AND HOBBES
by WATTERSON

OLLY-WOLLY POLLIWOGGY UMP-BUMP FIZZ!

HEY!

HA HA! I STOLE YOUR FLAG!

BUT I HIT YOU WITH THE CALVIN BALL! YOU HAVE TO PUT THE FLAG BACK AND SING THE "I'M VERY SORRY" SONG!

I DON'T HAVE TO SING THE SONG! I WAS IN THE "NO SONG" ZONE!

NO YOU WEREN'T. I TOUCHED THE "OPPOSITE POLE", SO THE "NO SONG ZONE" IS NOW A "SONG ZONE"!

I DIDN'T SEE YOU TOUCH THE OPPOSITE POLE! YOU HAVE TO DECLARE IT!

I DECLARED IT OPPOSITELY BY NOT DECLARING IT. START SINGING.

"HERE'S THE 'VERY SORRY SONGG'. WON'T YOU HELP AND SING ALONGG?"

BUM BUM BUM

I BLEW IT! I KNEW IT! I'M VERY VERY SORRY THAT I TOOK YOUR PRECIOUS FLAAGGG!

HE'S SORRY! SO SORRY! JUST DON'T DO IT ANY MORE, YOU SCURVY SCALAWAAGGG!

I'M FREE! I GET FREE PASSAGE TO WICKET FIVE!

NO, THAT'S WHAT WE DID LAST TIME, REMEMBER?

OH YEAH. HMM.

OK, THE NEW RULE IS WE HAVE TO JUMP EVERYWHERE UNTIL SOMEONE FINDS THE BONUS BOX!

THAT'S GOOD!

THE ONLY PERMANENT RULE IN CALVINBALL IS THAT YOU CAN'T PLAY IT THE SAME WAY TWICE!

THE SCORE IS STILL Q TO 12!

WATTERSON

Calvin and Hobbes by WATTERSON

ANOTHER PLANET, ANOTHER SWEEPING PANORAMA OF INDESCRIBABLE GRANDEUR!

THE INCREDIBLE SPACEMAN SPIFF ZOOMS TO THE SURFACE OF AHNOOIE-4!

TOUCHING DOWN, OUR HERO SETS OFF TO SEARCH FOR SENTIENT LIFE!

ALAS, SPACEMAN SPIFF ONLY DISCOVERS A HIDEOUS BLOB SO MONUMENTALLY STUPID THAT IT JUST STARES STRAIGHT AHEAD, COMPLETELY UNAWARE OF ANYTHING AROUND IT!

COMPASSIONATELY, OUR HERO DECIDES TO PUT THE BLOB OUT OF ITS MISERY. SPIFF SETS HIS BLASTER ON "LIQUEFY."

EWW! MISS WORMWOOD! CALVIN'S SHOOTING SPIT BALLS!

PERPLEXED BY THE BLOB'S RESILIENCE, SPIFF ADDS MORE JUICE AND PREPARES TO FIRE AGAIN!

WATTERSON

UFOs! ARE THEY REAL?? HAVE THEY LANDED IN OUR TOWNS AND NEIGHBORHOODS?

DO THE CHILLING PHOTOGRAPHS BY AN AMATEUR PHOTOGRAPHER REALLY SHOW A SINISTER ALIEN SPACESHIP AND THE GRIM RESULTS OF A CLOSE ENCOUNTER, OR ARE THE PICTURES AN ELABORATE HOAX?

LISTEN TO AN EXPERT ON SPACE ALIENS SPECULATE ON THEIR HIDEOUS BIOLOGY AND THEIR HORRIFYING WEAPONRY! ALL THIS AND MORE...

...ON CALVIN'S SHOW AND TELL ... NEXT!

CALVIN, WILL YOU COME HERE PLEASE?

TWITCHING TUFTED TAIL, A TOASTY, TAWNY TUMMY: A TIRED TIGER.

...AN ALLITERATIVE HAIKU BY CALVIN. THANK YOU, THANK YOU.

SHEESH.

YOU KNOW HOW PEOPLE LOOK AT MODERN ART AND ALWAYS SAY, "MY 6-YEAR-OLD KID COULD DO THAT!"?

WELL, THAT GAVE ME THIS GREAT IDEA! I'VE DECIDED TO BECOME A FORGER AND GET RICH PASSING OFF FAKE PAINTINGS TO MUSEUMS!

A LOT OF PAINTINGS SELL FOR TENS OF MILLIONS OF DOLLARS NOW, SO I MAKE A PRETTY GOOD HOURLY RATE.

YOU SHOULD PROBABLY SCRATCH OUT THE COPYRIGHT DATE ON THE CARTOON STATIONERY.

OOH YEAH, GLAD YOU CAUGHT THAT!

CALVIN AND HOBBES

by WATTERSON

HISTORICAL MARKER "CALVIN'S HOUSE" IN JANUARY, SOME 40 SNOWMEN MET a GRUESOME FATE ON THIS SPOT.

EVERY DAY I LOOK FOR A MOVING VAN HERE.

KNOCK KNOCK

GREAT MOONS OF NEPTUNE! A FOOL MORTAL FEMALE!

CALVIN?

I'M NOT CALVIN! I'M *STUPENDOUS MAN!* FRIEND OF FREEDOM! OPPONENT OF OPPRESSION!

UH HUH. WHAT ARE YOU DOING?

I WAS JUST ABOUT TO USE MY STUPENDOUS POWERS TO LIBERATE SOME COOKIES BEING HELD HOSTAGE ON THE TOP SHELF OF THE PANTRY! NOW IF YOU'LL EXCUSE ME, DUTY CALLS!

SLAM!

A BOLT OF CRIMSON STREAKS ACROSS THE SKY! THE MAN OF MEGA-MIGHT IS OFF TO SAVE THE DAY!

DID THEY HAVE AN EGG YOU COULD BORROW?

NO ONE WAS HOME, MOM.

calvin and hobbes

by WATTERSON

MY LIFE COULD BE A LOT BETTER THAN IT IS.

I'M HAPPY, BUT IT'S NOT LIKE I'M **ECSTATIC**.

LIFE IS LIKE TOPOGRAPHY, HOBBES. THERE ARE SUMMITS OF HAPPINESS AND SUCCESS...

...FLAT STRETCHES OF BORING ROUTINE...

...AND VALLEYS OF FRUSTRATION AND FAILURE.

BUT *I'M* DEDICATING MYSELF TO EXPERIENCING ONLY **PEAKS**! I WANT MY LIFE TO BE ONE NEVER ENDING ASCENSION!

EACH MINUTE OF EVERY DAY SHOULD BRING ME GREATER JOY THAN THE PREVIOUS MINUTE!

I SHOULD ALWAYS BE SAYING, "MY LIFE IS BETTER THAN I EVER IMAGINED IT WOULD BE, AND IT'S ONLY GOING TO IMPROVE."

I'M JUST GOING TO JUMP FROM PEAK TO PEAK! I'M... WHOOPS.

AT LEAST WITH FLAT PLACES, YOU DON'T HAVE SO FAR TO GO DOWN.

ONLY **LOSERS** GO DOWN! FOR ME IT'S ONLY GOING TO BE **UP** AND **UP**!

CLICK.

PANDER TO ME!

PLAYING A RECORD? I'LL SHOW YOU SOMETHING INTERESTING.

COMPARE A POINT ON THE LABEL WITH A POINT ON THE RECORD'S OUTER EDGE. THEY BOTH MAKE A COMPLETE CIRCLE IN THE SAME AMOUNT OF TIME, RIGHT?

YEAH...

BUT THE POINT ON THE RECORD'S EDGE HAS TO MAKE A BIGGER CIRCLE IN THE SAME TIME, SO IT GOES FASTER. SEE, TWO POINTS ON ONE DISK MOVE AT TWO SPEEDS, EVEN THOUGH THEY BOTH MAKE THE SAME REVOLUTIONS PER MINUTE!

ON YOUR MARK... GET SET... GO!

I'M GOING SO SLOW, I'M MOVING BACKWARD! I'M WINNING!

THAT'S CHEATING!

CALVIN and HOBBES

by WATTERSON

UH-O...

OH NO! EVERYTHING HAS SUDDENLY TURNED NEO-CUBIST!

IT ALL STARTED WHEN CALVIN ENGAGED HIS DAD IN A MINOR DEBATE! SOON CALVIN COULD SEE BOTH SIDES OF THE ISSUE! THEN POOR CALVIN BEGAN TO SEE BOTH SIDES OF *EVERY*THING!

THE TRADITIONAL SINGLE VIEWPOINT HAS BEEN ABANDONED! PERSPECTIVE HAS BEEN FRACTURED!

THE MULTIPLE VIEWS PROVIDE TOO MUCH INFORMATION! IT'S IMPOSSIBLE TO MOVE! CALVIN QUICKLY TRIES TO ELIMINATE ALL BUT ONE PERSPECTIVE!

IT WORKS! THE WORLD FALLS INTO A RECOGNIZABLE ORDER!

YOU'RE STILL WRONG, DAD.

IS IT TIME FOR SNACKS YET?

HOBBES, WE'RE TRAVELING AT LIGHT SPEED THROUGH AN INTERDIMENSIONAL CONTINUUM LAPSE! WAIT TILL WE LAND!

OK, I'LL JUST INVENTORY THE SNACKS AND RECORD THEM IN THE JOURNAL.

YOU *COULD* HELP ME DRIVE, YOU KNOW! IF WE MISS OUR EXIT, WE COULD FLY RIGHT INTO THE BIG BANG!

WHAT WOULD HAPPEN THEN?

THERE'D BE NO UNIVERSE, AND PROBABLY NO TIME!

I THINK WE SHOULD EAT THE SNACKS *NOW*.

SIT STILL, WILL YOU? YOU'LL MAKE ME SWERVE.

THERE'S A DIPLODOCUS! WE'RE IN THE JURASSIC! WE MADE IT!

UGH. I CAN'T BELIEVE YOU WANTED TO COME BACK HERE.

LAST TIME WE DIDN'T BRING A CAMERA.

ALL WE NEED ARE A FEW GOOD DINOSAUR PHOTOS AND WE'LL BE RICH WHEN WE GET HOME.

IF WE GET IN NATIONAL GEOGRAPHIC, MAYBE I'LL GET TO MEET SOME OF THOSE TIGRESS BABES THEY SHOWED IN THE APRIL ISSUE! YOW WOW!

THOSE WERE FEMALES? REALLY, I DON'T KNOW HOW YOU CAN EVEN TELL THE DIFFERENCE.

HEY! HERE'S A CHANCE TO GET A PICTURE OF SOME STEGOSAURS!

SEE, THESE PHOTOS WILL ANSWER HUNDREDS OF QUESTIONS ABOUT DINOSAUR ANATOMY AND BEHAVIOR! PALEONTOLOGISTS WILL PAY THROUGH THE NOSE TO SEE THESE!

TAKE A PICTURE OF THIS ONE. HE'S SMILING.

JUST A MINUTE. JUST A MINUTE.